The Wealth Garden

CATCHING BUTTERFLIES
WITHOUT A NET

Presented by Matthew Newnham & JP Parker

Yinspire Media
info@yinspiremedia.com
www.YinspireMedia.com

ISBN 978-0-9819708-4-4

Editorial Director: AJ Harper
Print Management: The Book Lab
Cover Design: Pearl Planet Designs
Book Design & Typesetting: Thomas Keppel

www.WealthGardenBook.com

Contents

Foreword

DR. TOPHER MORRISON

Imagine that you've just been dropped in the middle of an uncharted desert. What would you do to survive and thrive? How much would you value a map and a compass to help you navigate through this unfamiliar terrain?

Business and economic climates can frequently appear like this — unfamiliar, even hostile. The route to success can often be unclear or unspoken. Under such conditions, you may be unsure about your optimum path or role. Having clear goals is essential, but understanding the route that's best suited for each of us is vital.

Having spent over twenty years studying, and helping thousands of people to get better results, I know firsthand the value of practical tools in helping to boost personal wealth-building performance—and what works in practice. I was introduced to Wealth Dynamics a little over two years ago, and since then, I've seen ample evidence of its power to highlight your strengths and identify your weaknesses—and do the same for your team and your business. Where Wealth Dynamics really scores is in its unique recognition of eight entrepreneurial types (called wealth profiles), and the guidance it provides on how to play to your strengths based on your personal profile.

As I share in my book, Settle for Excellence (Stop Chasing Perfection), there is no magic solution that works for everyone, every time. I have found that Wealth Dynamics provides an excellent map, with your wealth profile acting as a personal compass, pointing the way to the most efficient route to wealth. In my case, this has enabled me to take my business to significant new levels, via strategies that are tuned specifically to my profile and my business.

Wealth Dynamics shares the sound scientific principles developed by Carl Jung. Over twenty thousand entrepreneurs worldwide have taken the online profile assessment, and this book contains real-life stories from thirty-four of them who apply Wealth Dynamics in their businesses. Several of these authors are friends of mine, and I know that the insights they have gained through Wealth Dynamics have made a tangible difference to their businesses. Finding and following our natural path in life is critical to playing at our highest level and making our greatest contribution.

The Wealth Garden is comprised of stories — excellent examples of a growing trend — in which those who are investing more in themselves to gain and apply practical insights will be best placed to take advantage of opportunities in any market condition.

Having clear goals is essential, but understanding the route that's best suited for each of us is vital.

In my experience, learning how to improve your own performance in all areas of life and taking the required actions to raise your game to the next level are the most crucial and valuable investments you can make. Wealth Dynamics has enabled me to produce tangibly better results, as it has for the authors in this book. My advice is to be open to what you can extract and put into practice to lift your performance and your business. Everything we do in life, we do, at the deepest level, to be happy. And happiness comes from acknowledging who we truly are — and acting on that truth.

So I invite you to learn from the stories in The Wealth Garden, take the online assessment to find out your own profile, and apply those strategies you find resonate most strongly with you.

And as you do, continue to take care, dare to dream and make each day an epic adventure!

Welcome to
The Wealth Garden

Roger Hamilton's *Your Life, Your Legacy*, has a section called "The Net and the Garden." In it, Roger describes the fundamental misunderstanding of wealth as something that we think we have to chase after in order to attain — a phenomenon akin to chasing butterflies in a garden with a net.

We can train ourselves to run faster, to acquire bigger and better nets, to develop new butterfly-catching and -keeping technologies; we can even become extremely proficient in all these skills. But no matter how expert we become, in this model we still have to get up every single day and run around with a net… until the day we simply drop from sheer exhaustion!

At the end of the day, real wealth isn't about our technology. It isn't even about our skills. It's about recognizing that there's a smarter way to go about this whole game. It's finally beginning to dawn on us that chasing after business may no longer be a viable strategy.

The global economic and entrepreneurial conversation is shifting now, as we ask ourselves: What if wealth is not about our ability with the net, after all? What if it's really about our ability to attract, like a garden filled with beautiful, scented flowers that naturally draw the butterflies?

Seen in this light, the questions change dramatically. The key question before us now is: How does our garden grow? How can we best engage authentically with our clients and customers so that further business is naturally attracted to us, like butterflies to a beautiful garden? And how do we keep those butterflies coming back — how do we invest our time, money and energy most effectively to build a consistent flow of wealth?

This is ultimately what Wealth Dynamics, the system that inspires and informs this book, is all about. Based on the ancient wisdom of the Chinese I Ching, Wealth Dynamics offers a simplified, modern framework that shows how each of us can tap into our unique path to value and wealth creation. That path is the focused and balanced application of our natural gifts and those of others to attract, rather than chase, the results we seek. The truth at the present moment is that most people simply don't know they can be gardeners instead of butterfly-chasers; in business and in life, and for a variety of reasons, they're not playing their natural game. Organizations whose teams understand this and are in tune with their natural game, as individuals and as a whole, will thrive, achieving better results more efficiently. Ventures where this is not the case will not fare as well, especially over time.

Wealth Dynamics shows us that once people move beyond old patterns and begin to constructively marry their natural skills, traits and talents, and then mesh smoothly with the rest of a team doing the same, each player generates greater value and higher levels of passion, authenticity and mutual respect. This in turn takes attraction to a whole new level, and defines our optimum path to creating value (and, ultimately, wealth) sustainably and ethically.

Our aim for *The Wealth Garden* is to shed light — via applied examples — on the creation of sustainable wealth through intelligent application of these centuries-old principles. We see this as a much-needed antidote to current approaches that are proving, all too dramatically, to be unsustainable.

Another key principle underpins this book. It is often observed that wealth is an inside job, a journey of self-discovery; and while this is true, in our experience it is not the full picture. Wealth is not only an inside job — it is also a job we do together, for ourselves and for the world. This is increasingly true in the 21st century, as our beautiful blue-green planet grows smaller and more intimate every day. As a case in point, this book is written by a truly international community of inspired and inspiring entrepreneurs. We've been extremely fortunate to be able to assemble such a group of global gardeners here. We come from every inhabited continent on the planet: Asia, Africa, the Americas, Europe and Australia; and from the rather significant islands of Hong Kong, New Zealand, the UK and Hawai'i.

We come from a wide diversity of life backgrounds and professional fields. But within this variety, we share a powerful common bond: we are all social entrepreneurs, each deeply motivated to create tremendous value through commerce while leveraging that value to serve the greater good of humanity and the planet. Our stories are gathered here to provide real-world illustrations of how the application of Wealth Dynamics moves us past our initial knowledge into deeper insights that empower us to generate lasting results.

At the end of the day, real wealth isn't about our technology. It isn't even about our skills. It's about recognizing that there's a smarter way to go about this whole game.

We offer this book as a foundational step on the wonderful journey into Wealth Dynamics, which we've each found to be a powerful tool in creating our own gardens. We've arranged the chapters of this book to follow the seasonal flow of Wealth Dynamics. You'll find stories that span a wide spectrum, representing well over five hundred years of combined business experience. Whether your focus is on corporate growth or solopreneurship, on the hard sciences or the gentle counseling arts, we trust that you will find a blend of information and inspiration within these pages that you can apply in your own business and life.

May these stories provide the insights that enable you to put down those nets at last, safe in the certain knowledge that you can attract a constant stream of butterflies — not to mention bees and hummingbirds! — to your own thriving garden.

We look forward to cultivating with you. Welcome to The Wealth Garden.

Matthew Newnham, Edinburgh
JP Parker, Los Angeles

Wealth Dynamics Primer

To know oneself is the first step toward making flow a part of one's entire life.
— Mihaly Csikszentmihalyi

Before former cell phone sales manager Paul Potts performed in the first round of the live television show "Britain's Got Talent," he said, "By day I sell mobile phones. My dream is to spend my life doing what I feel I was born to do." Paul's rendition of the aria *Nessun Dorma* stunned the judges, and brought the audience, two thousand strong, to their feet in a tumultuous, collective standing ovation. A few weeks later, Paul won the entire competition, and his life was transformed. His first opera album sold more than two million copies in six months, getting airplay in more than fifteen countries, and his 2008 concert tour spanned twenty-three countries in ninety-seven concerts.

Paul hasn't achieved success without work, but his singing is about more than the simple application of talent. Paul says his voice has always been his friend, and he feels he was born to sing. And when he does, he enters into what athletes call being "in the zone," also known as a state of flow: total immersion in an activity that is challenging and intrinsically worthwhile, in which time seems to stand still.

We are happiest and achieve the most when our actions are in tune with our natural gifts and talents. When we tap into our flow, we achieve more, with far less apparent effort—and a great deal more enjoyment. By contrast, we've all seen people who spend months, years and even an entire lifetime working very far away from their natural state of flow. And though it's possible to turn in a winning performance under such conditions, this requires a level of effort that can rarely be sustained for more than brief periods without creating increased stress and compensatory behaviors. Many of us are out of alignment and we don't know why; or we may know why, but don't know what to do about it.

If what we're doing feels as though we're swimming upstream, chances are we're out of flow. The concept of flow has been around in different guises for centuries, and while it's most often associated with sports performance and creativity, the term "flow" was introduced to Western psychology by Professor Mihaly Csikszentmihalyi, whose research in the 1980s highlighted how working in a "flow state" could increase productivity, even in repetitive tasks such as assembly-line work. Since then, there have been many attempts at describing how flow can be harnessed in business.

Wealth Dynamics is a profiling system created specifically for entrepreneurs and their teams, to apply the concept of flow in a practical way to business. It's based on the I Ching, the ancient Chinese text that inspired Swiss psychiatrist Carl Jung to develop his concepts of psychological types. Jung's work laid the foundations for personality profiling tools that are increasingly used in business, such as the Myers-Briggs Type Indicator, MMPI and DISC.

Wealth Dynamics shows how each of us aligns most naturally with one of eight wealth profiles describing a personal path to accessing and maintaining flow in business and personal relationships. As you read the following summaries of these profiles, you may recognize your own traits and those of colleagues, friends and family members.

The **CREATOR** profile: Generates new products, services and businesses, or transforms existing ones; sees and maps the possible; blazes the trail

The **STAR** profile: Shapes and amplifies a unique brand and message; takes the stage; shines a light on the message; generates excitement

The **SUPPORTER** profile: Leads and motivates the team that makes it all happen; recognizes, honors and brings out the best in people; enrolls and energizes with enthusiasm

The **DEAL MAKER** profile: Connects people and projects; orchestrates deals and alliances by bringing the right elements together at the right time, in the right place; loves to play host and be where it's all happening

The **TRADER** profile: Moves the best deals through the marketplace, turning them into assets; finds resources and nurtures ongoing relationships; serves as a touchstone for what's real

The **ACCUMULATOR** profile: Collects valuable assets (including intellectual property); analyzes and archives relevant data and materials; willingly, patiently waits for reward; keeps projects on track and on time

The **LORD** profile: Consolidates and controls cash flow; uncovers hidden financial value; streamlines and systemizes processes for efficiency

The **MECHANIC** profile: Creates better systems; fine tunes processes to replicate and scale them up; improves effectiveness and measurable outcomes

You can choose to play any game, of course; but why not play your game — the one that brings you the best results and the most fulfillment? While each of us can (and does) express the qualities of several of these profiles, the strong tendency will be to act most often in line with our primary profile, and, to a lesser extent, our two secondary profiles (which in the vast majority of cases are those to the immediate left and right of our primary profile).

This Wealth Profile diagram gives us the relationship between the eight wealth profiles:

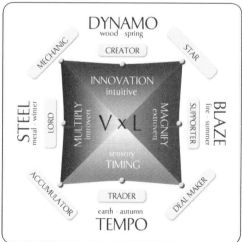

The Wealth Dynamics profile report, which you receive when you take the online Wealth Dynamics profile assessment, explains these concepts in much greater detail. Visit *The Wealth Garden* website at www.TheWealthGarden.com to learn more and find out how to get your own profile. Having your own profile results at hand will add even more relevance to the stories you'll be reading in the chapters that follow.

And as powerful as Wealth Dynamics can be when applied well, we offer the following advice, based on our practical experience:

- Our profiles don't define our personalities, dictate our life choices or magically make success happen.
- We view your profile not as a way of defining *who* you are, but rather, *how* you are — in other words, how you operate most naturally and authentically.
- Within this context, Wealth Dynamics provides valuable insights that can save you time, money and energy, both individually and in teams.

Ultimately, flow is about immersion in challenging activities that are intrinsically worthwhile, that bring out the best in us. Whether your path involves a dramatic career change — as Paul Potts's did — or re-energizing what you already do, we invite you to step into your natural flow, realize your full potential and make a lasting contribution.

Finding and Keeping the Magic

MIKE SOUTHON

The great golfer Gary Player took some issue with the notion of pure luck, and so do I. After he sank a thirty-foot putt to win a major tournament, someone told him it was a lucky shot. He agreed, but added, tellingly: "The harder I practice, the luckier I get." The same is absolutely true about entrepreneurship.

Successful entrepreneurship is not about the merits of your business idea. Ultimately it comes down to being in the right place, at the right time, with the right team. If you do have that magic you will be successful. Afterwards, people will say you were lucky; but in reality, you made your own fortune. Magic in business is about knowing how to increase your chances of success by following some simple rules to build the right team. This is a skill that can be learned and requires constant practice, just like putting.

The first key to successful entrepreneurship is to understand yourself and acknowledge that you are not perfect. In an article I wrote for my column in the *Financial Times*, I explained that many people decide to become entrepreneurs because they have come to the conclusion that they are essentially unemployable. Many were "let go" from their last place of employment and resolved that from that point forward, they could work only for themselves. This is all well and good, but in order for their businesses to succeed, they have to understand and address their character flaws, the ones that got them terminated in the first place.

To be a magical entrepreneur, the first thing you need is to find out exactly who you are, and therefore the other person you need to work with: someone with an opposite but complementary set of skills, your foil. The profiling tools of Wealth Dynamics are perfect for this; I use Wealth Dynamics every single day when mentoring entrepreneurs. It is only after you understand and acknowledge who you are that you can understand your ideal place in an organization. Then, you need to concentrate on your specific role as much as possible, and find someone else to work on those aspects of business you find difficult or time-consuming.

For example, a successful business needs to cover three key areas: sales, delivery and finance. A successful start-up usually has an extrovert responsible for the key ingredient in entrepreneurial magic: sales. The business will typically also have someone more introverted to be responsible for the delivery of the product or service. In the Wealth Dynamics model, if entrepreneurs are extrovert Stars, they should look for an introvert Mechanic; if they are Mechanics, they should find a Star. In both cases they are ensuring that the first two ingredients are covered, sales and delivery.

To be a magical entrepreneur, the first thing you need is to find out exactly who you are, and therefore the other person you need to work with: someone with an opposite but complementary set of skills, your foil.

Once you start generating revenue, you have to look after the third area, finance. You need someone who is good with numbers, spreadsheets, cash and cash-flow. In the Wealth Dynamics model, this is often a Lord or Accumulator; for example, a bookkeeper or accountant who can be engaged on a part-time basis in the early days, when cash is tight. Success in business is all about timing and teamwork. Once businesses have their sales, delivery and finance bases covered, the Stars can get to work creating attraction for their product or service — but it is crucial that they recognize what the market is telling them. This is the part of magic that is all about timing, something that Stars and Mechanics are often very bad at; they want success *now*, but the time may not be right.

For example, I worked for one start-up for six months trying to sell their software. My friends in the industry were quite interested in finding out more about the product, but for some reason would not buy it. Even harder was trying to sell the product to complete strangers. Rather than trying to address the root cause of the problem, I just kept trying to sell the product, and six months later, having sold nothing, I was fired. I was selling the wrong thing at the wrong time, but that was not the real issue. The problem was that I did not accept that I was selling the wrong thing at the wrong time.

Successful entrepreneurs always have a good foil.

Stars need to create attraction quickly; if they are unable to do so, they need to report back immediately and explain that, for some reason, the product or service is not getting the attraction that was expected, and the Mechanic can change something. If a Star and a Mechanic work together as an effective team, they can prototype new ideas very quickly in this way.

Successful entrepreneurs always have a good foil. A great example of an entrepreneur working well with his foil is Shaylesh Patel, the founder of Healthy Planet. Shaylesh was an accountant for Ernst & Young, and in 2001 he became the Chief Financial Officer for Flight Centre (UK) Limited. He was instrumental in helping the company grow its commission base from eleven million to twenty-two million pounds, but he did not want to be an accountant for the rest of his life. Shaylesh wanted to do something to help save the planet for his children. As a Star profile, it was natural that he teamed up with a great Mechanic, a geographer, as his foil. Together they pinpointed areas of the world that need adopting in order to rescue their ecosystems, and then made a deal with Google Earth to be able to display that data on the web.

The result is Healthy Planet, a successful social enterprise that allows people to pick one of fifteen thousand parks plotted around the world and give money to support its activities. If Shaylesh had remained an accountant the rest of his life, he would have ended up frustrated and bored. Now he is a thriving Star, clearly happiest when creating attraction for his company. All I did when mentoring him was point him in the right direction and explain how he could work better with his foil and further build his team.

Once you have the basis for a profitable business, you can start building your team. If the entrepreneur and foil are delivering a profitable product or service, and there is increasing demand from the marketplace, then they can begin to seek out other profiles to complete their team. In my case, I was already working with a great Mechanic, Chris West, who is co-author of our books and is responsible for the systemization and maintenance of the intellectual property of our business.

All Wealth Dynamics profiles have a yin and yang, a good side and a dark side.

But the first major learning I received from Roger Hamilton was that, as a Star profile, I also needed someone to negotiate my personal speaking fees. At first I was confused by this; all my life I had been in sales and consider myself an expert negotiator. Roger explained that, when Stars talk about money for their own services, they reduce the value of the brand. This was a major breakthrough for me, and I immediately hired a good friend to act as my Deal Maker. The whole process of talking about money is more pleasurable for her than it is for me, so she always gets higher fees for a speaking engagement than I would. Customers also have a better experience with her than they would with me; they always tell me how much they enjoyed working with her and how easy she made the process. She is better at finessing the whole deal, and since I hired her, my speaking business is much more effective and profitable. The final member of my team is my wife, an expert Accumulator, who makes sure all the money that is coming in does not go straight out again. She is also expert at filling in my tax returns and ensuring my business administration is what it should be.

All Wealth Dynamics profiles have a yin and yang, a good side and a dark side. For example, Creators are excellent at generating good ideas, but often they have too many different ideas and do poorly with finishing what they start. Stars are very radiant and create attraction, but can also be vain and egocentric. Supporters can turn into stalkers, insisting that you will be in their network whether you want to be or not. An unscrupulous Deal Maker will only propose a one-sided deal, not a genuine win-win for both parties. Traders are good at managing large numbers of similar transitions, but can become compulsive gamblers, addicted to the next throw of the dice.

A poor Accumulator is like Charles Dickens's character Scrooge: living in poverty, but with a fortune hidden away somewhere. A Lord who has lost touch with the reality of business knows the price of everything but the value of nothing, only buying the cheapest product or service, regardless of value for money. Mechanics left to their own devices will never finish anything; the product or service always needs new features, regardless of what the market actually wants — which is usually simplicity. Entrepreneurs need to be aware of this. It is easy to celebrate the good side of their profiles, but they need to be vigilant against slipping into the negative side, either through over-confidence when things are going well or negative behavior when things are going badly.

The model I use with all aspiring entrepreneurs is that they should go to the nearest pub or coffee bar with some friends and write down their elevator pitch on a coaster or cocktail napkin. You cannot fit pages of management jargon or complicated business models onto a piece of cardboard about four inches square.

Then, the next thing you do, even before you write a business plan or spend any money, is to find a mentor. In our model, as in my own life, mentoring has always been extremely important. After many years' business experience, having been advised by some great mentors, I am now an entrepreneur mentor myself, explaining to people the simple rules for starting and growing their businesses.

Entrepreneurs need to be aware of this. It is easy to celebrate the good side of their profiles, but they need to be vigilant against slipping into the negative side.

But you are always learning; in our best-selling book, The Beermat Entrepreneur, I suggested that psychometric tests were less than effective in selecting your team. But I have since realized that Wealth Dynamics has worked well for me personally, and so I now use it as a mentoring tool as well as to develop my own business. The Wealth Dynamics model has made me a better mentor. If you are successful, you will have the opportunity to become a mentor yourself. When you are young, older people mentor you, but as you grow older you increasingly find yourself advising other people, such as your children. Being asked to become a business mentor can happen very quickly if you have a sudden success, such as selling your business; that's what happened to me. It has taken me twenty years to fully develop my mentoring toolset, and today, I advise entrepreneurs on how to have a magical business. I also show them how to develop their skills to be mentors themselves, one day.

Finally, it is important to note that sometimes the magic just simply is not there. In that case, the entrepreneur is probably in the wrong place at the wrong time, and it is time to try something else. Even if you are successful, the magic can get lost over time, as entrepreneurs are often easily bored. When I notice successful entrepreneurs who have become unfulfilled or bored, I suggest they consider selling the business to the staff, taking a break, and then looking for a brand new opportunity.

The point is that magic in a business is never a fluke; Gary Player sinking a long putt was never just "lucky." Of course, he missed a lot of long putts — in the same way that we may miss the mark in our businesses now and then. The successful putts he made were after practicing diligently for hours. You can indeed get magic in your business, by constantly learning all you can learn and then applying those lessons in fresh new ways.

Mike Southon co-founded, built and sold his own company in the 80s and worked on seventeen different start-ups in the 90s (two later went public, three went broke!). He is now the UK's leading entrepreneur mentor. Mike is co-author of several best-selling business books, including The Beermat Entrepreneur and Sales on a Beermat, and he has a weekly column, My Business, in the Financial Times. Mike is an experienced conference facilitator and moderator, having interviewed over one hundred top business people for his own website, and is a Visiting Fellow in Innovation and Entrepreneurship at London South Bank University. He has made frequent appearances on television and radio, and delivers over one hundred presentations every year, all over the world. For more information on Mike and his business, please visit www.beermat.biz.

Rocking to a Better Bigger

MIKE HANDCOCK

Bigger isn't always better. For years, I was a general manager at a large financial services company. I was really good at it, and I made good money doing it, but I didn't enjoy it at all. Wealth Dynamics has taught me that that job was a Lord's job — and I'm not a Lord. I didn't know this at the time, though. I only knew that I wasn't excited to get up and go to work each day, even though my life was getting bigger — financially, at least.

Bigger doesn't always mean what we think it means. It doesn't always mean biggest. Our businesses can still be called successful, even if we're not Donald Trump. As authors, our books can be good and useful, even if they don't sell a million copies. And our fitness can show great improvement, even if we're not ready to run the Boston Marathon. Not everyone has to have the goal of saving the world. My focus is on helping all of us play a bigger game in our lives. For some people, that means simply getting home in time to read their kids a story.

My business, Rock Your Life, is dedicated to being the world's number one team of transformational leaders; we want to create the most transformational visionaries to assist the world in improving the environment, spreading education, reducing poverty and more. We're already in the top five, operating in seven countries. And we've been around for less than four years. Our success is not a freakish accident, though I haven't always been terrific in business. Before founding Rock Your Life, I left my job as a general manager at that financial services company and started two businesses. One was a construction company, which I hated and which wasn't doing well. The other was a realty company, and it wasn't thriving either because I never got a thrill out of selling anything.

Then, in 2004, I did my Wealth Dynamics profile. When I first looked at the profile square I believed I was a Star, but was worried I would come out a Creator. Well, I did come out a Star, both in 2004, when I was failing at two businesses that did not fulfill me, and also in 2007, when I was succeeding in a business I loved and had decided to do my profile again. The profiles were exactly identical; not one percent of difference.

The key to the profile is to do it on the basis of who you think you are, not what you are doing at the moment. People who get skewed results do it based on what they are doing, not what they *want* to be doing. I had a real "Aha!" moment with the areas *around* my profile. Above the line, people are strongly intuitive. Below the line, they have a strong sense of timing. I've never had a good sense of timing. I'm the only financial planner I know of who put money in the market three weeks before it crashed, and I finally asked my girlfriend to marry me three weeks after she dumped me. "You're a bit late," she said.

> *Not everyone has to have the goal of saving the world. My focus is on helping all of us play a bigger game in our lives. For some people, that means simply getting home in time to read their kids a story.*

But my intuitive side is strong, and I realized that whenever I've made my best decisions, I've done so by ignoring everything I learned from my educational experience. School taught me to wait, to study, to process, but for those of us above the line, it's gut instinct we need to follow. For years, my gut instinct and Star inclinations had been tamped down by society at large.

There are different types of Star profiles, but generally speaking, Stars are the most gregarious of all the profiles. They're the loudest, look-at-me type of people. But when you are five years old and a Star, the last thing your parents want you to do is act out, and your entire subsequent educational process seems bent on repressing the Star within. That repression never stops. When I was in financial services, I was the only Star among nine Lords. I was always being told to sit down and that my ideas were way too out there. This repression is the world's conditioning against our true selves, and this is where Wealth Dynamics can be a real eye-opener. We often see someone who, from the outside, seems to be an analytical person, but then his profile comes out as Star. It doesn't seem to fit, but that's probably because the person has been conditioned out of being a Star due to family or societal pressures.

Wealth Dynamics is so different from personality profiles, which tell people how they interact with the world. Wealth Dynamics tells people how they operate in the world. It enables them to understand what their true natural game is. That was certainly the case with me. I spent fifteen years trying to get to the top of the corporate life, only to discover that I didn't like it. Then I built my own businesses thinking, "This will make a lot of money," but I was overworked because I was out of profile. My corporate job was a Lord's job; my construction company was meant for a Mechanic and my realty business was meant for a Deal Maker. But I was a Star.

When I discovered my profile, I immediately got rid of my construction company. As for the realty company, I stepped out and brought in partners to run it, and in the next twelve months I made more from that company than I had in all the years I was running it on my own. The company literally tripled its earnings, and I went from working eighty hours per week to less than one.

But it was also time to figure out what to do next. I had just learned that people who enjoy what they do match their passions with their ultimate competencies, their unique abilities. I was a good speaker, a good writer and a competent musician. And I had an interest in helping others better themselves. From all of that, I created the Rock Your Life brand.

Rock Your Life is an organization of global experts in all areas of health, wealth and wisdom. These experts show you how to play a much bigger game in any area you wish, anything from sales and marketing to health and spirituality. So "bigger" is an individual thing. Bigger for you could mean you want a better diet; you want to have more influence on your family or you want to save Zimbabwe. Ultimately, though, it's really about focusing people, through a whole range of media and life events, to an actual understanding that there is a bigger reason why they are here.

My business is all about collaboration. First is the collaboration between us and a client. I'm an expert in only one or two things, but Rock Your Life is creating a group that covers the entire 360 degrees of someone's life needs, be they health advice, business advice, ways to brand better or sell better and so on.

There's also the collaboration within the business itself, between me and my employees and partners. Whenever I look to employ somebody, I don't hire a person; I hire a profile. When CVs and resumés come in, I read them to gauge, within one or two profiles, what the prospective employees are. Then I narrow them down to exact profiles. If a person is not the profile I want, she will not get the job. My team is made up of a number of Wealth Dynamics profiles, all in their proper roles. One of the beauties of Wealth Dynamics is that it gives me the freedom to let go of the things I'm not good at — things I once felt guilty about because others around me were so much better at them.

Wealth Dynamics is so different from personality profiles, which tell people how they interact with the world. Wealth Dynamics tells people how they operate in the world. It enables them to understand what their true natural game is.

For example, last year we wanted to franchise an aspect of the company. We knew we needed Lords. Our accountant was a Creator, but we needed someone who could explain how the numbers worked. I told her we couldn't use her anymore, and she knew Wealth Dynamics, so she said, "Okay." She then found us a Lord who could speak to the banks that were lending people money to invest in our franchise company.

Finding the right profile for the job was also essential to our social responsibility efforts. Rock Your Life does a ton of charity work, especially in India, but we had no systems for all those charities. Activity depended upon my time and energy, so I knew we needed to automate. We hired a Mechanic interested in social betterment who set up our systems, and now there is a stable flow of cash to our charity projects. Not so incidentally or coincidentally, every single person on my team asked to be part of the team. Because I was so rooted in my Star profile, I was attracting the right people.

One of the most common mistakes people make is not having anything to do with elements of their business that are not aligned with their profiles. People think that because they're Creators, they don't have to know the numbers, and a year later they're broke. Someone does my books, which go to my accountant. Then, every week, I am updated. In other words, I don't put the numbers together, but I know what's happening.

Every single person on my team asked to be part of the team. Because I was so rooted in my Star profile, I was attracting the right people.

Wealth Dynamics has changed my life. The moment of wealth creation for the Star is when he knows what he is. Not all Stars know what they are. For a long time I didn't. But once I did, things changed. Another of my biggest moments of wealth creation came when I realized I didn't want to run a traditional company. I didn't want to be in business; I wanted to play with people.

But to do that, and to play my own, bigger game, I needed all the profiles surrounding me. Playing that bigger game is not just knowing yourself; it's also knowing those around you. It's all about having the right balance of people on your team to attract everyone you need to succeed. And because of Wealth Dynamics, that balance is much easier to attain than I ever thought possible.

Mike Handcock is an innovator, creator, professional speaker and musician. He joined the financial services industry at the age of twenty-one and held numerous positions in it, including senior management in New Zealand's largest financial services organization. He has won numerous industry awards, as well as the "Inspirational Speaker of the Year" and "Businessperson of the Year" Awards. In addition, President Clinton recently cited Mike for his work in India and Cambodia with the SAGE Foundation.

Founder of Rock Your Life, Mike currently owns numerous businesses and has a passion for coaching and training. He is a sought-after international speaker and is the author of seven books released in Asia Pacific, two of them bestsellers. Mike has another book forthcoming. As a musician, he has played on nine CDs, four of them solo albums. For more information about Mike and Rock Your Life, visit www.RockYourLife.net.

Breathe Life
into Your Dreams

DR. JOANNA MARTIN

The day I left the hospital, everyone thought I was a lunatic. After graduating medical school with first class honors, I survived my first grueling year as an intern. My career was taking off. My future was set. It was all in front of me — a rewarding career in a respected profession, financial security, success — but I wanted out. I wanted something else — something that, unlike a career in medicine, offered an uncertain future: I wanted to act, to perform. But who trades in a bright, hard-earned future for a dream like that?

When I was eight years old, my uncle asked me what I wanted to do when I grew up. He mentioned that his daughter, my cousin, wanted to be a pediatrician, which he explained was a "doctor for kids." I thought that sounded like a good thing, so at age eight I told everyone I wanted to be a pediatrician. Children want to be a lot of different things: astronauts, teachers, movie stars, chefs, racecar drivers. My announcement could have been just one in a series of proclamations, had I not received such positive feedback from my parents (both pharmacists) and my grandmother (a nurse). They never pressured me to follow through with it; but their encouragement was reason enough for me to pursue that path.

So even after I fell in love with acting in high school, I still followed through with my plan to become a physician. Believing I would be satisfied exploring drama as a hobby, I set aside my secret desire to attend drama school. When I start something I have to finish it, so I found my way through six years of medical school at the University of Tasmania. Ironically, I was given two prizes: the Keith Millingen Prize for clinical skills and the GE Clemons Prize for the student who "most strongly exhibits the qualities of humanity, conscientiousness and devotion to the profession of medicine." Devotion? Ha! My dream of drama school all but forgotten, I was frustrated with my lack of passion for my field. It wasn't that I hated medicine; I just didn't love it.

Standing in that hospital room, I thought, "What if you actually did it? What if you followed your heart?"

One day, while working on the oncology ward at the hospital, my favorite patient died. She was a little pixie of an Irish woman, only eight years older than me. And as I looked at her I thought, "That could have been me." I watched her entire family gather around her, and I wondered: if I had been given the same prognosis, if I only had six months to live, would I still be a doctor? The answer came to me immediately. "No way." Standing in that hospital room, I thought, "What if you actually did it? What if you followed your heart?"

Right then and there I made the first deliberate, conscious choice of my life. This moment marked a true shift in the way I led my life from then on. I had denied my true nature for far too long — now there would be no more delaying of dreams, no more postponement of happiness. No matter how silly or risky it seemed, I would follow my heart. That night, as I listened to soothing music and sipped a glass of wine, I promised myself that by the end of the year I would either have directed a play or auditioned for drama school. Being a true overachiever, I did both! Everything that happened after that day was easy, because I was finally on the right path. I was in flow — my passion was rooted in my innate abilities — and so, as my dear departed Irish patient might have said, the road came up to meet me.

The drama school was the Actors Centre Australia — and it was pure heaven. At this forward-thinking school, I was introduced to the field of personal development. It seemed the perfect venue for me, and so in my spare time I embarked on a career as a coach and trainer for individuals and businesses. My career took off and eventually demanded my full-time attention. I went on to enjoy a successful (albeit hectic) professional life, working for one of the top personal development companies in the world. After a few years, though, I was exhausted from the long hours and the traveling. And I missed my partner, Greg. So I took nine months off to get my bearings.

It was during this time that I first came across Wealth Dynamics. Coming out a Star on the Wealth Dynamics profile test confirmed that my gut instincts were spot on, that I was right to pursue a career that involved some aspect of performance. As I delved deeper into Wealth Dynamics, I realized what being a Star profile is really about for me. What comes naturally to me doesn't come naturally to everyone. And the stuff I hate to do, other people love. I had been living according to my Star profile by instinct alone, but it wasn't until I studied Wealth Dynamics that I came to value my natural talents and proclivities.

I wanted something else — something that, unlike a career in medicine, offered an uncertain future: I wanted to act, to perform. But who trades in a bright, hard-earned future for a dream like that?

I had given up a career that didn't suit me, yet I still labored over the tasks and responsibilities that didn't come naturally to me, such as finance. You see, I thought that if it wasn't hard work, then I didn't deserve to succeed. Wealth Dynamics helped me to realize the error of my ways, and in giving up those details I was able to shift from a self-employed mentality to that of a business owner. Once Greg (a Lord) and I understood our profiles, we sat down and set goals for ourselves. But we didn't write down figures or specifics; we set goals about the flavor of our life. We created a "Lifestyle Design."

The exploration of Wealth Dynamics gave me a heightened level of self-awareness. It was as if doors had been blown wide open, revealing a path to profound happiness paved with conscious choice and deliberate intention. The thing is, even those of us who are bold enough to jump off the cliff to pursue our dreams may still end up unfulfilled.

How? Sometimes when people take that leap, they assume that a sacrifice must be made in order to realize their vision. They fall in love with the idea of their goal and tolerate a less than fabulous life as long as they're "following their dream." They willingly give up balance, contentment and even happiness, believing it is a small price to pay for reaching their goal. But true freedom can only be achieved through appreciation of the path and consideration of all aspects of life, of lifestyle.

I had made the leap for my passion but I was still searching, wondering why I was not in love with my life. Wasn't I following my heart? Wasn't that what life was about? Discovering my Star profile gave me insight into what was possible for my whole life. So rather than build a life around a business, or even our dreams, Greg and I came up with business ideas to fulfill our lifestyle criteria. For us, that looked like the creation of a number of educational businesses, which allowed us to travel the world and live our ideal lifestyle.

Once Greg (a Lord) and I understood our profiles, we sat down and set goals for ourselves. But we didn't write down figures or specifics; we set goals about the flavor of our life. We created a "Lifestyle Design."

Never before has there been a better time for people to create their own dream lifestyle. Technology has made it possible for people to live, work, play, build, grow and give from almost anywhere in the world. The only limitation is our imagination. It breaks my heart that people are stuck in jobs that they can't wait to leave, and that those who are going for their dreams accept unhappiness in their pursuit. People need inspiration and information, and so Greg and I created ShiftLifestyle.com to match lifestyle-centric business owners with the resources they need to succeed on their terms, to breathe life into their dreams.

Trading in my medical career for an uncertain future was a move made on pure instinct. When I boarded the boat to leave my native Tasmania for the uncharted waters of drama school in Sydney, I felt a calm I had never experienced before. I was not excited in a buzzy way, but in a deeply profound manner. As the crew pulled the ropes off the pier I thought, "This is the beginning of the rest of my life." Awakening to a new perspective through Wealth Dynamics gave me the same feeling.

If you "ended up" in your profession by way of influence of family or peers, by accident, or, as in my case, because of a knee-jerk reaction to a casual suggestion, you may harbor your own deep desires for something else. Something different. Something wonderful. You may not even know what it is. But maybe it's time to ask yourself the same question that allowed me to breathe life into my own dreams: What if you actually followed your heart?

An internationally acclaimed speaker and sought-after educator, Joanna Martin has taught over forty-thousand people on three continents. Combining her passion for performance with her coaching expertise, Joanna trained entrepreneurs and professionals in key communication, leadership and presentation skills, and consulted for companies such as ANZ Bank, John Fairfax Publishing and eBay. After three years as head trainer for the Christopher Howard Companies, she launched www.ShiftSpeakerTraining.com to help speakers achieve financial freedom.

In 2009, with her partner Greg, Joanna launched www.ShiftLifestyle.com, a community providing strategy and support for business owners who want a lifestyle, not just a living. Joanna is the author of Our Internet Secrets and her next book, The Lifestyle Shift, will be published in 2010.

The Time Is Now

BEA BENKOVA

One of the defining moments in my life was when my mother was diagnosed with cancer. Her response to the news staggered me and will always stay vivid in my memory. "Why now, when I've finally let go and have time to live my life?" she said to the doctor. "Why now?"

A successful woman, my mother had focused almost exclusively on business and family; no time to stop and really think about what she loved doing. The diagnosis cut so deep in part because she was not truly fulfilled. My mother thought she was at a new beginning — only to find out it was too late. She had instead come to a sudden end.

I was raised to believe I could do anything. As my natural inclination was always to see things from a bird's eye view, choosing to study macroeconomic and monetary policy felt natural, too. With a banking career in the financial center of London, I thought I was living a truly successful life, fulfilling my dream. Three years later, I received the devastating news about my mother. As my sister and I began the journey to help our mother heal, I recognized her life as my own, and her regret as my predictable future.

So many of us spend our lives climbing a ladder, only to discover it is leaning against the wrong wall. I wanted to begin the process of creating and living a fulfilling life — now. In exploring transformation, I began attracting healers, psychics, people who work with energy. Even at a workshop for entrepreneurs, I would find myself sitting between a psychic and a Reiki healer. As I began to work with energy, everything shifted, and I started vibrating at much higher levels.

Soon it became apparent that I had to leave investment banking and find a path with higher-frequency energy.

I knew I wanted to do something completely different, and although I had no idea what it was, I believed wholeheartedly in synchronicity. I was certain that if I had the courage to make the leap, then my path would be revealed. And it was. Just one month after I left the corporate world I met Roger Hamilton. His inspiring introduction to Wealth Dynamics spoke directly to my heart. Paradoxically, I had just left an industry solely focused on building wealth and here I was learning how to create true wealth for the first time!

So many of us spend our lives climbing a ladder, only to discover it is leaning against the wrong wall. I wanted to begin the process of creating and living a fulfilling life — now.

I learned that true wealth lies in our power to give and receive at our full potential. And from that I understood that building my true wealth was an obligation, not just an opportunity.

This is a unique time for women. We are coming to the foreground again and have the ability to make a huge difference on this planet. In the corporate world I knew so many women who were trying to realize their full potential and genuinely contribute, but they were merely emulating men. Running on adrenaline, they were frequently tired, unfulfilled and disconnected from their true selves as women.

As I studied Wealth Dynamics and my Star profile, I realized the difference I could make to humanity and to women. In a critical moment I got crystal clear about what I wanted to do and how to do it. To impact humanity, I would be a catalyst for extraordinary women who are taking the lead. I would create an environment around them so they are empowered to realize their full poten-tial — so that they can change the world. And I knew that if I wanted to attract women who are committed to making a difference, I needed to make a shift in my own life. As I undertook this transformation, Ararêtama Vibrational Es-sences created by Sandra Epstein became an integral support in the process.

As a Star profile, I first had to create my identity. It took me a year to develop my unique self, clearing old energy, creating space and gaining further clarity about the type of women I wanted to work with. I chose to attract successful women who are living accomplished lives but are seeking a deeper level of fulfillment — women who want to play a bigger game and make a major contribution to our planet.

My true purpose as a Star is to shine light on others. It begins with a conversation in which I guide women to connect with who they truly are. When each woman is ready, I connect her with the partners, experts and resources she needs to fully come into her own, to fulfill her vision and purpose. Once a client's purpose is clear, I stand for that purpose wholly, ensuring that everything in her life — her business, family and other relationships — is in line with that purpose. Everything in life is interconnected, and so I am like a guardian, a catalyst for her empowerment to become who she was *always meant to be.*

Since I stepped into my own light I have attracted many extraordinary women as clients, across all sectors, industries and backgrounds. Drawing on my background, skill set and intuition, I work with each individual client to refine her purpose, raise her vibration levels and recalibrate her life.

My true purpose as a Star is to shine light on others. It begins with a conversation in which I guide women to connect with who they truly are. When each woman is ready, I connect her with the partners, experts and resources she needs to fully come into her own, to fulfill her vision and purpose.

Along with Wealth Dynamics, I feel privileged to integrate Ararêtama into my work. I use an exclusive line of Sandra's Essences created for the Extraordinary Women in my network, which works at three distinct levels. First, whatever needs to be transformed for each woman taking the essences is brought to consciousness. Then, as if by magic, striking synchronicities happen within the community of women taking the essences. Finally, working with clarity and synchronicity, each woman connects to her purpose at the deepest level — expressing her unique legacy. Bespoke Ararêtama programs support them in moving forward with velocity.

Recently, I started working with Julia, an acclaimed fashion designer who, despite being very motivated and driven, was struggling financially. She loved painting and communing with nature but had little time to, as she put it, "indulge" in such pursuits.

A Creator profile whose natural state was one of high creativity, she was bogged down with managerial and fiscal duties. Julia was giving up her power — and her favorite tasks and activities — in an effort to master the areas that were not natural to her. She was out of balance, out of flow. Coming into your own, getting into flow, is a multi-layered process. I work holistically, considering all aspects of a woman's life and illuminating areas that need to shift and in what sequence.

When the shift occurs, as it did for me when I discovered Wealth Dynamics, it opens up unseen possibilities.

Using Wealth Dynamics we looked at which aspects of her business Julia could delegate, and soon she hired a managing director to handle day-to-day operations. She also took Ararêtama Creator profile essences to accelerate the progress she wanted to make both emotionally and creatively. I noted that for Julia, painting served as a form of meditation, and yet she viewed her painting time as a luxury. Creating an "energetic space" for her authentic self and deepest desires, I urged Julia to make painting a priority.

As she opened up to devoting precious time to her great love, Julia gained insight and began to experience synchronistic moments. She tuned in to the perfect time to make a phone call or launch a new marketing strategy. She found she was able to achieve more while doing less. Her sales increased, as did her salary. Our work is ongoing, but Julia is now operating in flow and has already reaped the greatest reward: she is standing in her own truth. From that truth Julia is on her path to attaining true wealth.

Sometimes people are not sure what their truth is, exactly. Even successful women need a shift in perception — from light bulb to laser beam, from the daily grind to the legacy they want to leave behind. The simple act of doing a Wealth Dynamics profile can bring on the shift because the discovery of one's unique identity empowers people to be true to themselves. When the shift occurs, as it did for me when I discovered Wealth Dynamics, it opens up unseen possibilities.

My aim is to give women both wings to fly and a safety net. In keeping with my purpose I have created a community — or constellation — of extraordinary women who seek to contribute to the good of humanity. The constellation operates at a very high frequency, creating one synchronistic opportunity after another. Each woman fully inhabits her own unique position related to her purpose. And it is the unique, purposeful position of each woman that creates the constellation.

As their ambassador, I connect my clients with other women who could propel their purpose forward. Being a part of the constellation enables women to take action immediately, to move faster, to progress in an elegant, harmonious way; they are empowered to take huge leaps — or first steps — before it's too late.

My mother's profound regret helped me realize that the best time to begin is now. Not when it seems most convenient, or when everyone else's needs are met, but now. If you are hungry for a life with more meaning, begin now. If you know you are more than the sum of your parts, begin now. If you sense that there is something new or greater possible for who you are and what you stand for, begin now. Just begin.

Bea Benkova is the Ambassador and Coach of Extraordinary Women and a Wealth Dynamics Master Practitioner based in London. She specializes in empowering women to develop their full potential and take a leading role not only in their own lives but also in creating positive shifts on a global scale. Her clients include prominent female entrepreneurs, business owners and managers, as well as actors, scientists and politicians across

Europe, the US and Asia. Originally from Slovakia, she studied at Oxford University and previously worked in the office of the Slovak Deputy Prime Minister and as a banker in the City of London. Learn more about Bea and her transformational programs for women at www.BeaBenkova.com.

Rewire Your Mindset...
and Your Life

PETRUS CARSTENS

My wife and I have a longstanding Thursday morning ritual: we head to our local coffee shop for a leisurely talk about our lives, our children and our future. Years ago, on one of these mornings, I asked my wife — off the cuff — "When do you want to retire?" I was so surprised when she replied, "In five years," that I nearly fell off my chair.

Retire in five years? On a minister's salary? I thought it was impossible. "What do you want to do after we retire?" I asked. She had this whole wonderful plan worked out: we'd buy a 4 x 4, travel throughout our native South Africa and other African countries and see what we could do to make a difference in the communities of our poorest neighbors.

Her vision resonated deeply in my soul. It inspired both of us so much that we decided to see if we couldn't accomplish it. So, on subsequent mornings at our coffee shop, we formulated a five-year plan to bring us to our goal. One thing was clear: we needed to build a solid financial foundation if we were to meet it.

As I began reading and educating myself about wealth and money, however, I realized that I would need to rewire my mindset in order to build the foundation for our dream. It dawned on me that although I had supported other people in their efforts to make money, I didn't personally value money. For me, the spiritual life had always been of the highest value. How was I to reconcile my spirituality — my foundation — with a pursuit of wealth, even if that pursuit was an altruistic one? Thus began my journey — a very rewarding one — of integrating spiritual power with material power.

Back when I was studying for a degree in economics, I felt empty; my pursuits seemed selfish. I wanted to do something greater in the world. This spiritual yearning led to six years of study in theology, after which I became a minister, serving a congregation of forty-five hundred for fifteen years. Through the church, I saw people with wonderful purpose and passion were working so hard to make a difference with very little money. My yearning, then, became to grow wealth in order to help these communities I cared about so much.

I had studied theology during Apartheid, a time when much violence occurred in impoverished areas. After two weeks of witness as part of a group doing community work in Crossroads squatter camp, I began sharing with all my friends the mindset I observed that kept people trapped in poverty — and which was confirmed time and again, as great efforts to make change in these environments fell apart. I saw how difficult it was for those who had been born into a culture of poverty to create a vision that was not ruled by poverty.

As I began reading and educating myself about wealth and money, however, I realized that I would need to rewire my mindset in order to build the foundation for our dream.

I started my own company, doing entrepreneurial development in such communities. The people we worked with did very well — until eventually, and seemingly inevitably, they would push an invisible self-destruct button and lose everything they had built up over two or three years. During this process, I never realized how trapped I was in the *middle class mindset*. But later, as I began work on the five-year plan my wife and I had created, the dualism within myself was revealed.

It was clear I was dealing with dueling beliefs and desires, a tension between the spiritual and the material that humans have wrestled with since the Greek philosophers. We think that money and spirit are somehow at odds, that we have to isolate ourselves from the world when we go on a spiritual journey — like

St. Simon Stylites, who lived on a tall pole in the desert to separate himself from the sinful world.

We struggle to integrate these two great powers, seeing money as the "root of all evil," labeling the rich "greedy" and referring to them as "stinking rich." But the truth is that money is an essential tool for supporting much of the work that flows through spirit. In fact, money is as spiritual as we want it to be. It encapsulates our labor, and in that sense it is the fruit of our souls.

I never realized how trapped I was in the middle class mindset. But later, as I began work on the five-year plan my wife and I had created, the dualism within myself was revealed.

Those who have integrated the spiritual and the material — the two most powerful driving forces in us as human beings — are the ones who have changed history. When I went through my own process of integrating these forces, I finally figured out what I wanted to do. In the process, the question that helped me was this: how could money support my spiritual pursuits? I answered this question for myself when I saw what kind of difference I wanted to make. Then I was ready to go out and make money in support of my vision. In changing my mindset, I got my mind set.

Wealth Dynamics is a great tool for helping us rewire our mindsets. It goes even deeper than showing us our most authentic desires and greatest talents, because it teaches us a holistic approach in which the spiritual and material are equally essential — just as each profile is essential to a whole and thriving venture.

Once I found my flow and my true path through this integration, our five-year plan to build the financial foundation for our future was achieved in three years.

And when that was accomplished, I saw that there is a real science to building wealth. I thought, "How could I take many people with me in this wealth creation journey?" I retired from the church so I could serve four-hundred-thousand people, not just the forty-five hundred in my congregation.

27

Investment intelligence, not opportunity, grows your wealth. And the biggest investment you can make is in your own education. I co-founded the Ample Workz Group and created the Financial Diamond Course to help people grow wealth sustainably and in community, so that circles of prosperity will continue to widen, rather than clamp down.

There are two worlds out there: the world of salary earners and small business owners, who learn to survive from month to month; and the world of those who know how to work with and grow their money.

As happens with those growing up in a culture of poverty, those who have learned to survive in the salary spectrum might take a lifetime to learn how to grow wealth. I understood that giving this course was not enough to help people learn how to invest. They also needed great teams to support them.

So I started investor Hubs, which work according to Wealth Dynamics profiles and principles. People attend the Diamond course, write a five-year investment plan and then become part of our investor Hub or partnership. Our due diligence team looks at hundreds of investment opportunities and chooses the best, then presents its studies to the Hubs for discussion.

Those who have integrated the spiritual and the material — the two most powerful driving forces in us as human beings — are the ones who have changed history.

That's when the magic starts happening. Each profile brings a different view to the debate. Supporters are the glue that brings the group together, making sure everyone is involved. Traders see how to leverage contracts, using their great sense of timing in buying low and selling high. Creators add value with their out-of-the box thinking, Stars through their enthusiasm and marketing skills. (Yet in the Hubs, Stars and Creators learn, for once, to shut up and listen). It's exhilarating to see people working together. Everyone's blind spots are covered. Hunting in a pack gives each member so much more power.

Our first Hub bought many properties and invested in cash-generating assets. Hubs multiply and share investment opportunities. Now, having established Hubs in South Africa, Australia and Singapore and shortly in countries throughout Asia, we're working on worldwide Hubs. You're pretty powerful when the whole world is your playing field; and each team member can play at any level and benefit from opportunities he wouldn't otherwise have access to. Being part of a Hub is the best risk management strategy you can have.

That's when the magic starts happening. Each profile brings a different view to the debate.

The values of Ample Workz and our Hubs echo those of Wealth Dynamics. Abundance of life, love and wealth is our core value. We teach what we live and live what we teach. We love what we do and do what we love. And we believe that all human beings already have what they need to create the life they want.

Retirement is not part of my vocabulary anymore. Instead, when my wife and I talk about our lives at the coffee shop, we look at them in five-year stages, determining how we'll build the steppingstones to where we want to go next. In five years we'll rewire again, and work full time in impoverished communities. Before that, I need to build a wealth foundation for myself. I have not forsaken my ultimate goal in doing so; it's always where I'm going.

That's why we don't call it retiring, but rewiring — setting yourself up with investments and a passive income source to support you as you bridge to your next career, forever finding more fulfilling ways and spending more time to do what you are most passionate about and through which you can express yourself authentically, integrating your spiritual and material power. Rewire to the next level. If you've got the vision, the support will present itself.

As minister of a large Dutch Reformed Congregation, Petrus Carstens met many people with wonderful visions for making a difference, but soon realized that without finances people are limited in accomplishing their goals. In 2004, Petrus started investing, and within two years he built up an asset base exceeding $2.4 million and doubled that in the next year. By 2006, he started his first company. That same year, he was the top-performing student globally in Robert Kiyosaki's (author of Rich Dad, Poor Dad) wealth coaching academy. He now owns ten companies with his partner, Charl Ackermann.

Petrus is the creator of the Financial Diamond Course and co-founder of the Ample Workz Group, a network of companies focused on empowering people to live the lives they want and gain the means to afford them. One of these companies, Ample Opportunities, maximizes investment returns through gearing and leveraging different streams of income for each investment opportunity. Its strategy is to "hunt in packs" and form strategic alliances to give investors access to opportunities that would otherwise only be accessible to the wealthiest. Petrus's vision is to contribute to the economic empowerment of the whole of Africa. To learn more about Petrus and his work, visit www.AmpleWealth.net and www.AmpleWealthEvents.com.

And It All
Came Tumbling Down

NICK HAINES

When I first met Mike he had just tried to commit suicide. A brilliant, highly-regarded fashion designer, Mike suffered from severe depression brought on by the loss of his business. For ten years Mike was one of the most prominent business leaders in his industry, running a profitable, well-managed, super-successful fashion house and factory. (I've changed the names and industry to protect privacy, but the story is true.)

Despite having a sound financial footing, a fantastic team and a stellar reputation, Mike's company had gone bust in the span of eighteen months, leaving Mike despondent and without hope. Perhaps failure opens up opportunities for self-awareness, jolting us awake from our stagnant slumber. But Mike was so lost, so oblivious. He really had no idea how it all came tumbling down.

If we can gain some insight into situations, it allows us to move and shift our perception; without it we can sometimes become fixed or stuck in the way we do or see things. At certain times we can fail to adapt and change as the world changes around us, just following old patterns and ways of being. Chinese philosophy and Wealth Dynamics can help us gain insights into this, breaking old patterns and moving forward.

Each Wealth Dynamics profile has a number of strengths but it also has a challenge, an Achilles' heel. The tricky part is, the challenge can keep changing at different times in our lives and can often be the flip side of a more positive aspect of our personality or profile, a strength that becomes a weakness. To use

31

myself as an example: as a Star profile with lots of Dynamo energy, I tend to have lots of ideas and drive. But this is also my challenge, because sometimes my ideas are not quite as brilliant as I imagine them to be, or it may not be appropriate to follow them through.

In the past, I would jump on every idea, launching one project after another. I fell into the challenge — the trap — of one of my profile's greatest strengths. By pursuing all of my ideas I was actually blocking my flow. I came to understand that in order to meet my challenge I need help, and so now I run new ideas by trusted friends and colleagues, often Supporter profiles. A little-appreciated value of good Supporters is that they tend to be good at helping filter ideas, sorting out what is worth keeping, developing, improving and what is not. In pausing and asking for feedback, I can differentiate the value and viability of my ideas.

Beautiful dreams and remarkable companies fall apart every day because people struggle to have insight about these complex challenges, and because they fail to change their approach or perception of the world. As a practitioner of Chinese medicine and philosophy, I have seen firsthand how imbalances can cause people to make brilliant moves or terrible decisions, resulting in resounding success or total disaster.

When Mike walked into my office nearly twenty years ago he could barely function. Completely broken and destroyed, Mike still lacked insight about his past choices and was totally out of balance. As I treated Mike for his depression and we talked about his business, the story gradually came out as to what had happened. Mike explained that siphoning off the creativity of young student designers was an accepted practice in the fashion industry. He knew what this felt like, having experienced the same process as a fashion student. When Mike started his own company he made a commitment to do the right thing, to pay student fashion designers very well, to give them credit for their designs, and to allow them to showcase those designs.

A Creator profile with Dynamo energy, Mike was very successful because he was a good designer, but also because he placed a high value on justice, a significant but often overlooked Dynamo trait. People with strong Dynamo energy also have a thing with rules; they make them, break them or play with them, sometimes to great effect. James Dyson, for example, broke the rules of vacuum design and created the first cyclone- and bagless-operated vacuum cleaner, eventually generating more than six billion dollars from his products. Mike also broke the rules and created justice — and a wildly successful fashion house.

When Dynamos break the rules it can be a huge win or a complete failure, and it is their flexibility that can determine their long-term success. For example, Richard Branson, the pioneer behind Virgin Atlantic Airlines, defied convention and built an empire. Napoleon Bonaparte, in an attempt to create his own empire, ignored the rules completely. Both Branson and Bonaparte made mistakes, but Branson has insight and flexibility about his Dynamo nature and so learns from his mistakes. Bonaparte was far more rigid with his plan, the Achilles' heel for many Dynamo types, and so on escaping from prison he restarted the war!

> *Each Wealth Dynamics profile has a number of*
> *strengths but it also has a challenge, an Achilles' heel.*

Mike's wife, Margaret, worked at the company as well. Most Supporters are really good at looking after people, and Margaret was no different. She made sure the interns and staff settled in well and had a positive work experience. Above all, with her Blaze energy, she was their fierce protector. This desire to protect, although not a well recognized Blaze trait, can often determine the success or failure of Supporters. The company quickly developed a reputation as a fantastic, fair place to work, and attracted the brightest, most talented student designers. Every year Mike and Margaret had their pick of hundreds of student applicants with their young minds and fresh ideas. It was a positive cycle. By virtue of his Dynamo energy and Creator profile, Mike was leveraging off other Creators, yielding brilliant results. In turn, they were leveraging off the experience of working with Mike.

With the support of Clive, a Trader profile focused on price and creating a quality product, and Chris, a Lord charged with focusing on the finances, Mike built a healthy, successful business. As a foursome, they worked very well together. And although they did not have the language of Wealth Dynamics to explain exactly why everything flowed so well, they understood that they were a perfect team, a well-oiled machine.

Then, in 1991, a recession hit the UK, and Mike came to a fork in the road. The big department stores renegotiated terms with their suppliers, typically asking for fifteen percent discount and ninety days to pay the invoice. These companies had tremendous power, and they knew most of Mike's fellow suppliers would accommodate them. Many Creators would react with outrage, but some would choose to raise their game instead, innovating to add value that they could leverage. Mike became stuck, seeing only one way or view; he believed the new deal was unfair, and in his unfaltering commitment to justice, he went too far.

> ### *His rigidity caused him to lose his biggest customers.*

Although Mike's company could easily afford to wait ninety days for payment, he knew that many of the smaller fashion houses could not. He thought if he could get these companies to unite and say no to the new terms, the department stores would cave in. He refused the terms on principle, but he was alone in his fight. As other suppliers went along with the big stores, Mike was left out on a limb with the contracts lost.

His rigidity caused him to lose his biggest customers. Once Mike made his decision, Margaret, Clive and Chris were faced with their own fork in the road. Giving in to her desire to protect others, Margaret let go of her ability to filter and dropped her ultimate role as a Supporter: marrying the grand plan with grounded reality to ensure it happened, profitably and sustainably. Margaret colluded with Mike and refused to lay off any staff. Before long the company started entering a financial winter burdened with a heavy staff bill and dramatically reduced revenue.

Clive, with his Tempo energy, desperately needed to understand why Mike and Margaret were destroying the company on a principle. He knew they had to keep the big department stores as clients. The situation baffled him and so he became angry and withdrawn. Chris, with his Steel energy, battled Mike and Margaret for a time, trying to keep the company from bankruptcy. When people with high Steel energy become stressed, their strengths of detachment and seeing what is missing become their challenge. Chris resigned shortly after they lost their big clients, taking with him the relationships with the banks and creditors.

The business went to the wall in eighteen months. Where the company once thrived with the team playing to its strengths, this disparate group was playing to what had become their weaknesses.

Mike's commitment to justice and breaking the rules served his company well for many years, attracting the best designers with the best ideas. But his strength was also his challenge, and when tested, he fell right into it, losing key customers and stopping the flow of new revenue. Margaret, with her earnest need to protect and support her staff, fell into her own trap, which ultimately drained the company's reserves.

Like lemmings blindly running toward a cliff, all four of them chose a path that led to the destruction of the company. Yet there was a different path available, several in fact, none of which involved the company failing. For example, Mike could have used his Dynamo energy to rally other industry players to create extra value for their big clients, resulting in a better deal. If Margaret had focused on protecting the staff by protecting the company first, perhaps in the end she would have been able to rehire her staff. Rather than withdraw and retreat, Clive and Chris could have smoothed over the damaged relationships with clients.

The business went to the wall in eighteen months. Where the company once thrived with the team playing to its strengths, this disparate group was playing to what had become their weaknesses.

When people are operating in profile and are properly balanced, they meet their challenge head on, adjusting their approach. For example, if Margaret were in balance she would have realized that sometimes you have to make some people unhappy to make other people happy. Clive, with his ability to understand the customers, would have questioned more to understand the situation. If Chris had risen to his challenge, he would have stayed connected longer and perhaps sorted out the finances.

When Mike came to see me for treatment of his depression, he was still totally and utterly convinced that he had been right to stand up to the big companies. Even after he watched his entire life's work go bust, he still hadn't made the connection between his fixation on justice and the demise of his company. I helped Mike to reflect on past events, and over time he was able to see that his strategy was not the only option. With new insight into self, Mike embarked on a new venture within the fashion industry, and succeeded.

When faced with your own fork in the road, a deeper insight helps you make better choices. When you are in balance, aware of your strengths and challenges, you are better equipped to create greatness.

Nick Haines is a practitioner of traditional Chinese medicine and philosophy with thirty years' experience. He has helped individuals and businesses create new opportunities and achieve profound results through integrating Chinese energetic theory within their lives and current projects. Nick shares the power and practical application of this philosophy in his DVD series, The Hidden Patterns of Conscious Wealth, and in his forthcoming book, Conscious Wealth and Patterns of Behavior.

Nick has been involved with entrepreneurial businesses all his working life. Understanding the need for an integrated health system, Nick founded a multidisciplinary complementary health center in 1987, which now has twenty-three practitioners. One of the first people in the United Kingdom to gain an MSc degree in acupuncture, he co-founded The Northern College of Acupuncture in 1988, and currently serves as the Chair of Directors. Nick served on the steering committee of a landmark social enterprise project in one of the most deprived areas in the UK and he lectures nationally and internationally on Conscious Wealth. To learn more about Nick visit www.Nicholas-Haines.com and www.Conscious-Wealth.com.

Coaching toward Lives
of Least Resistance

BERT VERDONCK

Here's the scenario: You're traveling to a tropical island for business or pleasure, say Bali. Unfortunately, your suitcase doesn't arrive, and at the Lost Luggage Desk you have difficulty describing your belongings. What's more, your wallet, which contained your passport, was stolen, so you can't even identify yourself. Is there anything you could have done to prepare for this nightmare situation?

Actually, there is. Most people now own digital cameras, so before leaving home you could have taken pictures of your suitcases and what was in them. You could also have taken pictures of your passport, driver's license, credit cards, etc. Then you could have e-mailed all of these pictures to yourself so that you could access and download them at any Internet café anywhere in the world (including Bali). This idea came easily to me because I'm a Creator, and that's what I do: I come up with ideas. But not everyone is a Creator, so coming up with that idea may not have been intuitive for many — in the same way that other things, like balancing books or ironing out logistics, are far from simple for me. Creators aren't the only people who come up with creative ideas, but coming up with innovations and solutions is our path of least resistance.

I didn't always know this. In fact, generating terrific, original ideas comes so easily and naturally for me that for a long time I assumed everyone had the ability to do it as consistently as I did. In addition, since coming up with good ideas was simple for me, I always found it difficult to ask to be paid for it. Therefore, I never made money doing what I was good at; I always earned a living doing jobs that felt the most like work.

It is very easy to underestimate what we're good at, since what we're good at comes so easily. The first step on the path of least resistance is to fully understand what it is you're good at. The next step on the path of least resistance is learning how to capitalize on what you're naturally good at. I now know that what I find so easy, other people find incredibly difficult. And I know how to make a nice living by focusing on my unique abilities. I've also learned how to ask others to help me in areas where I simply do not belong. Because of that knowledge, I'm walking happily down the path of least resistance, enjoying life.

I used to run a company that worked with different suppliers in delivering services to customers. About five years ago, while at this job, I did my Wealth Dynamics profile and found I was a Creator. This pretty much confirmed everything I'd thought about myself. But even with this new knowledge, I persisted as CEO of the delivery company.

It is very easy to underestimate what we're good at, since what we're good at comes so easily. The first step on the path of least resistance is to fully understand what it is you're good at. The next step on the path of least resistance is learning how to capitalize on what you're naturally good at.

In 2007, my wife was undergoing serious surgery, so I took some time off to reflect upon my life. I came to the conclusion that I was unhappy a good eighty percent of the time, largely because, as CEO, I was constantly performing tasks not suited to me. For instance, I would spend hours poring over spreadsheets, and I am most certainly not a numbers person. I decided that I wanted to focus on creating new ideas, solving problems and helping people achieve more. And the way to do that, I realized, was through "life hacking" — finding shortcuts to get the same results with less effort, or better results with the same effort. I even had a name for it: Genius Shortcuts. But how could I transform this into income?

That same year, I took thirty-one days to walk eight hundred kilometers of El Camino de Santiago, the ancient pilgrimage route through southern France and northern Spain. On that journey, I encountered many people who asked me, "What do you do?" For the fun of it, I responded, "What do you think I do?" Most of them said I was a life coach, or a coach of some kind. It seemed I was destined to become one. So I got some training and learned how to be a coach. Now, as a coach, I life hack for others — helping them to find their shortcuts, their own paths of least resistance. I always thought life coaches should be psychologists, or have medical backgrounds. But my ability to generate original ideas and implement them in the lives of others makes life coaching quite natural for me.

I have learned that it's better to delegate to others who are more competent in their field of expertise and focus more on the areas where I am really exceptional.

And I set up my own management team, keeping in mind what I'd learned through Wealth Dynamics and adhering to it. I'd always thought, for instance, that it was empowering to be a CEO because as CEO, you are in charge. But in my case, it was actually limiting to think I should be a CEO, running everything. I have learned that it's better to delegate to others who are more competent in their field of expertise and focus more on the areas where I am really exceptional.

When I coach others, I work in three phases — create, connect, contribute. First, I create clarity as to what they want in life and why they are here. To do this, I use the Wealth Dynamics profile to discover who they really are. Because of my training, I have a pretty good sense of what someone's Wealth Dynamics profile is after spending a few minutes with him. I confirm this with the Wealth Dynamics test report. At first, the Wealth Dynamics profile seems like a simple test, but when you dig into it, you understand that it has fantastic layers underneath. It's so simple and easy to implement, and I've learned that each Wealth Dynamics profile is perfect for those who match that profile. Everyone is unique, but everyone has a profile that fits. There is no right or wrong; it's all about one's path of least resistance.

The second phase of coaching is the connect phase. This is when I connect a client to her vision and to other people. Every person's primary profile has complementary profiles he works particularly well with. These profiles maximize each other's value and leverage with each other. After explaining these dynamics, I look into my own network to make valuable connections for my clients.

The contribute phase comes last. Because of modern technology, a great shift is occurring in the world. It's staggering to contemplate, but it's also magical. I ask my clients to find ways to contribute to this great shift, and help make the world a better place. I personally give ten percent of everything I make to charity. I do believe that by letting go and giving, we get what we want. So far, I've been really blessed with this coaching formula, not only because it's been effective in helping others, but also because the formula works as effectively for individuals as it does for groups.

Each profile has its keys to communication , but these keys are useless until everyone in a team knows his own profile and the profiles of each of his teammates.

Laura, one of my coaching clients, has a management function with a multinational company, but it's not where she belongs. She always used to create in an artsy sort of way, but when I did her profile, we discovered she's a Star. Thus, her forte isn't creating — but once something has been created, she's great at making it more attractive, especially when it's her own product. So she hired me, a Creator, to come up with ideas for her products. Then she leveraged those ideas to make more attractive products. Her first workshop was so successful that she's planning two more. Laura used to be so unhappy in her work, but now she's working on creating more cash flow so she can fully devote herself to what she loves. She is in the process of changing her own destiny — a remarkable thing to be able to do.

The groups I'm most often asked to help are management teams. So often, terrible communication exists between members of a team — usually because they simply don't understand themselves or each other. They also don't understand the real issues between them, and in the end they get angry and can't work together.

For instance, many entrepreneurs are Creators. A Creator develops a good business, and it grows, so she attracts an exceptional salesperson, who is very often a Star profile. When people with these profiles are not in a natural "flow state," working together can result in a destructive clash of egos and constant fighting. I coach these partners to see the value that each profile brings, and the particular way in which each profile relates best to others, so they can work together in flow and maximize their combined value. Each profile has its keys to communication , but these keys are useless until everyone in a team knows his own profile and the profiles of each of his teammates.

I'm amazed by the wisdom of Wealth Dynamics. I'd long dreamed of creating an audio CD about Genius Shortcuts, and last year at the Wealth Dynamics Master Practitioner Conference, I put Wealth Dynamics to the test again. I first talked with other Creators about what the product should be, then I went to Stars to talk about creating attraction to the product. Having worked in the communications industry, I was skeptical about what the Stars could bring to the table, but I was blown away by their suggestions. I talked with a Supporter about identifying my potential audience, to a Dealmaker about partnerships, to a Lord and Accumulator about pricing and margins, and finally to a Mechanic about the logistical challenges involved in selling the CDs. One night, for me, reaffirmed the lifetime of wisdom available through Wealth Dynamics.

Since I began my journey with Wealth Dynamics, following my own path of least resistance, I have gone from working one hundred and fifteen hours per week to sixty, and I'm close to getting that down to forty. My income has increased by thirty percent, and about ninety percent of the time I really enjoy what I do — which is the greatest gift of all. I never dreamed that such material and spiritual rewards could be found along the easiest of paths. But in fact, that is where they always were.

Bert Verdonck is an entrepreneur and life coach with a background in Internet technology, biometrics and communication. Working in several corporate functions, he discovered that understanding people's needs, connecting them and staying on top of cutting edge technology are key elements for successful management. To that he adds the component of "Genius Shortcuts," which he uses to help people, teams and companies simplify their lives and their ways of doing business. He's a frequently invited keynote speaker and broadcasts his own radio show on life hacking. To learn more about Bert, visit www.BertVerdonck.com

Equip Your Dream

MARGARET HAMAR

My father could have died wealthy, but he didn't. He struggled financially his entire life, and when he left this earth he possessed no material wealth, nothing at all. It wasn't because he was incompetent or unlucky — it was because he never understood who he was, or what constituted real wealth. My father was a mechanic, and a very fine one. (Had he ever done his Wealth Dynamics profile, he would probably have been a Mechanic in that context, too.) But he had some old-fashioned notions about making money, so it never dawned on him to use has abilities as a mechanic to get wealthy.

Dad believed the rich got richer and the poor got poorer, and the way to get rich was to work hard and make a lot of money. Once you acquired some money, you simply used it to make more. Dad was always busy making money, trying to get rich, but he was constantly using the wrong means to do so. My whole life I watched him start business after business, each of them falling flat. Once he had a used car business. I was sitting in his office when the phone rang. The caller asked about a car that had been advertised. "It's gone," Dad said, and hung up. Even at that young age I realized he had no idea how to be a salesman. He also had no *desire* to be one. If he could have repaired the cars and had someone else sell them and someone else keep the books, that business could have been a roaring success.

Being passionate about what you do and clear about your purpose in life are crucial to creating wealth. Once you have that passion and clarity, you can always amass more money — no matter how much you lose. My mom was like my dad in many ways. Of the eight Wealth Dynamics profiles, she was probably an Accumulator. She saved up what money came her way and couldn't imagine how to capitalize on any opportunity to get more. Considering how hard my parents worked, they should have died billionaires.

For years, I was headed down the same path. I worked hard and attended a number of seminars on moneymaking strategy, but got nowhere with them. The problem is, many seminars teach us techniques we're not naturally suited to use. Their leaders advocate avenues that they are naturally suited to travel. Of course methods suited to them work for them, but they won't necessarily work for everyone.

As children, we discover pretty quickly what we're good at — but then forget, through years of being told to apply ourselves to activities we not only don't like to do, but aren't very good at, either. So most people, by the time they reach adulthood, no longer know what they're truly good at. They follow many different paths in pursuit of wealth, changing jobs, attending countless seminars — and generally getting lost in a seemingly endless maze. It is nearly impossible to create wealth without having a deep understanding of who you really are.

Being passionate about what you do and clear about your purpose in life are crucial to creating wealth. Once you have that passion and clarity, you can always amass more money — no matter how much you lose.

As a psychologist, I understand that there are many factors that contribute to individual makeup. Our experiences and our past relationships are essential to our self-knowledge. Wealth Dynamics, however, brings to light the deepest and most profound essence of who we are. This knowledge is fundamental, foundational; if we don't understand ourselves, we cannot enjoy good, healthy relationships of any kind.

One of my clients, Jane, ran a retail business with her husband. Their business and personal relationships were okay, but could have been better. When

Jane hired staff, she would expect them to be jacks-of-all-trades, doing sales, paperwork, everything. One particular employee was an introvert. She loved doing paperwork, but she hated doing sales. This made for uncomfortable friction between her and Jane. There was a lot of tension between Jane and her husband, too. He was a natural salesman. All day long he was out front, interacting with customers, which to Jane seemed like doing nothing. What's more, she was a natural saver, while he was a plunger. He often came up with big ideas for investments, but when she pointed out their flaws, he thought she was being negative and resented her for holding him back.

The key is getting your relationships right, which you can't do until you understand who you are. Once your relationships are solid and healthy, business and wealth creation will follow, in flow.

For years, Jane read books and attended seminars on wealth creation strategies, but nothing worked. Among the mass of conflicting wealth creation information out there, no method will work if it's not suited to you. For Jane, the struggle to succeed didn't add up, especially since she was a hard worker. Then she came to see me. Once she understood her Wealth Dynamics profile, everything made sense.

The key is getting your relationships right, which you can't do until you understand who you are. Once your relationships are solid and healthy, business and wealth creation will follow, in flow. Through Wealth Dynamics, Jane and her husband came to understand themselves better. They realized they each had distinctive talents that could benefit their business. They also came to understand each other better. She learned that he wanted to feel more significant, and he saw that she wanted to feel more connected and safe. Ultimately, they were better able to meet each other's needs, both personally and professionally. They also came to see others more clearly.

When employers are scouting for a new hire, they often choose a "go-getter," or someone who is like them. But if you need someone to do accounts, you don't want a go-getter, you want an introvert. Understanding this helped Jane hire the right people for the right jobs. As a result, she and her employees are much happier. When you are building a team, you need to make use of your team members' natural strengths. Doing what they're naturally good at, people will do it better — and faster — than anyone else. Because they're doing it better and faster, they're happier and their productivity is higher. The team as a whole is a lot more motivated, collaborative and dynamic than it would be if each person were doing a job he was unsuited to.

> *Many of the struggles in our lives are directly related to the gap between who we think we are and who we really are. In order for those struggles to disappear, we must first learn who we are.*

Many bosses hire the wrong person for a job — as Jane used to. And after all the time and energy they expend training this person, she quits six months later, unsatisfied with her job. When people know what their profiles are, when they know where they belong, it makes everything easier. Knowing each team member's profile shortcut Jane's team-building process: she knew what she needed and who could meet each need. People feel better about their jobs when they know their own value to the team; they also feel better about the team when they understand the value of each teammate.

Jane has gained the confidence to make important financial decisions in line with her wealth creation profile. And she's found that understanding herself has impacted not only her business and finances, but every sphere of her life, leading to greater overall fulfillment.

Another client, Susan, came to see me because she felt completely stuck. Wealth creation eluded her, and she hated her job as a personal assistant. She got paid quite well, so she couldn't understand why she hated her job so much (as she had many others). We did her Wealth Dynamics profile, and she turned out to be a Creator, which was not at all conducive to the work she was doing. I thought Susan would be excited to learn the truth about herself, but when I told her she was a Creator, she looked devastated, shocked. "I want to be a

Star," she said, almost whispering. "You can still be a Star," I consoled her. "But your natural talent is for innovation." That did not cheer her up. She thanked me quietly, then grabbed her purse and dragged herself out of my office as dejected as if she'd just found out her fiancé wanted to call off the wedding.

Many of the struggles in our lives are directly related to the gap between who we think we are and who we really are. In order for those struggles to disappear, we must first learn who we are. For the next three months Susan was very quiet with me, reluctant to talk. Then one sunny spring morning, during a breakfast I was hosting for people I'd profiled, she came bounding in and said, "I am in flow." She explained that she finally accepted that she was a Creator, and when she did, amazing opportunities presented themselves to her, ones perfectly in line with what she wanted to do. "I want to decorate houses," she told me. "I walk into a room and I can see the possibilities." Before Susan understood herself, she took jobs she wasn't suited for. That's why they felt like such hard work. Once she knew who she was, and accepted herself, Susan's world opened up. The way to wealth is along the avenue best suited to your natural talents. If what you're doing is too hard or makes you miserable, you're doing the wrong thing.

> *The way to wealth is along the avenue best suited to your natural talents. If what you're doing is too hard or makes you miserable, you're doing the wrong thing.*

I often wonder what could have been for my parents, had they been able to apply Wealth Dynamics to their lives. If my father had lived long enough, he would have found his flow. He died in a place called Lightning Ridge, a remote spot in the outback of New South Wales, Australia. He'd gone there to mine for opals. When we got word that he'd died, my sister and I decided to make the difficult journey there to bury him. I paid for the funeral.

There were so many bush fires that most of the roads and train lines had been closed. So we flew in a small plane to a nearby town, where we rented a car and drove the rest of the way. On that drive, we dodged more kangaroos than I'd ever seen before. Once we got to Lightning Ridge, and I collected Dad's final possessions, I discovered he had some of the right tools. But he didn't really know how to use all of them. Rather than give the job of cutting the opals to someone who knew how to use the tools, he did it himself, losing a lot of opals and a lot of money in the process. It hit me that that was the perfect metaphor for his life: he never had the right tools and the right team to support him. He didn't even know what the all the right tools were, or what the right team was.

That's where Wealth Dynamics comes in. It shows us the core of who we are, fully equipping us to choose the right tools for our own wealth creation. Those tools then allow us to fast-track our paths to success in every possible realm — relationships, teams, wealth creation, communication — leading to a life of greater fulfillment and quality.

Every morning I wake up fully energized, and eternally grateful that I get to spend my day doing what I love to do — helping others get to where they too spend their days doing what they love. I cannot imagine how any of that could have been possible without Wealth Dynamics.

Margaret Hamar, BA, Postgraduate Diploma In Psychology, MAPS, is a psychologist who has followed her passion for empowering others to be the best they can be, to help them tap their true potential and optimize their performance in life. A Master Practitioner, she uses Wealth Dynamics through her business Your Wealth Key to bring others into better relationship with themselves and others (www.YourWealthKey.com).

Wearing the Right Hat

HELEN BICHEL

For fifteen years I was a successful entrepreneur, enjoying a level of accomplishment many others strive for and never attain. There was only one problem — I was tired, frustrated and miserable.

Very hands-on from day one, I ran myself ragged developing two businesses, one a nursing recruitment company, the other a home nursing service. Not only did I create the businesses, I also managed them and had my fingers in marketing, sales and recruiting. I was so busy, trying to do everything!

I ran on adrenaline and was exhausted. I put in twelve-hour days at the office, sometimes on weekends, and that doesn't count all the hours I spent on the phone at home after I closed up shop. Worst of all, I was terribly unhappy. I didn't get to spend nearly as much time as I would have liked with my family and friends, and in the end I was deriving no great joy or satisfaction from the job itself. Financially, my businesses were successful. But that "success" brought me no real degree of happiness, personally or professionally. Life was hectic, and I was coming home from work drained, every day.

Frustrated and tired, I decided to sell my businesses. Shortly afterward, I discovered Wealth Dynamics, and soon all the misery of my previous fifteen years made sense. I was invited to attend a seminar with Roger Hamilton — an introduction to Wealth Dynamics profiling. Roger's presentation really resonated with me, and I realized why I'd been having such a hard time running my two businesses. After doing my Wealth Dynamics profile, I learned that I was a Creator. That's why running the businesses took a lot of my energy and didn't come naturally to me. I loved inspiring my team and sharing all the big picture ideas I had to develop the businesses, and I loved creating the strategies and processes, but I kept finding myself doing the day-to-day activities too. Managing a business and a team is definitely not my natural flow as a Creator.

My team couldn't have been much happier coming to work than I was. A Creator likes to continue creating, so I was constantly coming up with new ways to do things and introducing new products. Often these ideas were still being implemented when I was already on to the next big thing. It was hard for all of us. I always had my creative hat on, which meant my team was constantly trying to catch up. For me, nothing could happen quickly enough — and my team was overwhelmed because everything kept changing!

Financially, my businesses were successful. But that "success" brought me no real degree of happiness, personally or professionally. Life was hectic, and I was coming home from work drained, every day.

After I learned about Wealth Dynamics, I saw the negative impact I created within my team dynamics. My team could have been much happier and more fulfilled, and I'm sure business performance could have been elevated too, had I focused on empowering them rather than constantly creating. After I discovered Wealth Dynamics, I spent a lot of time exploring the team aspect of leadership. I was trying to work out how I could take what I learned in Wealth Dynamics and effectively transfer that knowledge to assist, support and empower individuals, teams and businesses.

I recruited new staff for some of my XL friends, using Wealth Dynamics profiling as part of the selection and team-building process. This proved highly successful and beneficial, and has become my new business — Wealth Recruitment Strategies.

Now my whole approach to running a business has changed. I am following Roger's eight stages of an enterprise, and have appointed a high-performing Supporter to be the company CEO. He is passionate about people's experiences in the workplace, and he is a natural connector who leads our team to success. He empowers everyone to fulfill their potential and enjoy the work experience.

I have absolutely nothing to do with the day-to-day management of the company. I am only involved in the vision, the expansion strategies and the big-picture planning. All our team members have been profiled and are working within their areas of expertise and natural flow based on the Wealth Dynamics profile frequency. And what is transpiring within my own business is what I aim to do globally for many other businesses.

Our business mission is about placing people in a position of natural flow, so that their full potential is harnessed to maximize benefits to themselves and their organizations. We work with our customers to deliberately create wealthy workplaces that are productive and harmonious for everyone, and we use Wealth Dynamics profiling as one of our tools for achieving this. We use our expertise in Wealth Dynamics profiling to impact all levels of a business from management to operational staff, improving performance, effectiveness, efficiency and each personal work experience.

Wealth Dynamics profiling allows us to discover problems that could very easily go undetected for an indefinite period of time, costing businesses an exorbitant sum in financial and human capital.

The first step in our process is getting really clear about leadership strategies, current performance and potential being reached within the client organization. We then review how each person is managing or being managed in the workplace, and whether he is engaged and committed to his role. We profile each team member and assess the fit based on performance and potential for that role within the workplace.

We also develop Key Success Indicators (KSIs) and introduce self-mastery and success management strategies. We look at each department and determine how much time is invested in generating sales, and how much time is spent managing systems, processes and back office activity, since each position must add value to the department and the organization. Furthermore, we work with the owner of the company or the business manager to identify what promises are being made to the company's team, customers and shareholders. When the organization is clear on its promises, it becomes more focused about what needs to be done in alignment with those promises and how to create the flow needed to achieve those goals.

It has been my experience that often owners are not clear why they are running their businesses in the first place. When that's the case, it is little wonder these businesses are hives of inefficient chaos being run by unhappy, busy people. During our business team review process, we identify the causes of loss or missed potential, the magnitude of that loss and the real impact it has on the business's people and bottom line. Once all this is identified, we assist in getting the team aligned and moving forward collectively to fulfill everyone's goals.

Everything we do is about putting the heart back into a business, and fully developing everyone's human potential within the company.

Let one of our client companies exemplify what improvements can be made and the value gained by profiling and integrating the concepts of team dynamics. The company had been in operation for twenty years, with a very stable work force. Our client had owned the company for five years, and had inherited the existing staff. It seemed to him that everybody was pretty happy and working well together. The business was growing steadily, but not achieving the level of growth he believed was possible.

When we profiled the entire team, the problem quickly became apparent: most of the sales team was introverted, reluctant to cold-call or visit new customers. We also discovered that the purchasing manager was the wrong profile for such a job, even though she'd been in that role for ten years.

As it happened, the purchasing manager moved on for personal reasons. A new manager was hired, based on the Wealth Dynamics. She does three times the work and everyone in the company is amazed at the results. Oddly enough, our client was actually happy with the old purchasing manager, and it wasn't until the new one came that he realized what he'd been enduring. Wealth Dynamics profiling allows us to discover people problems that could very easily go undetected for an indefinite period of time, costing businesses an exorbitant sum in financial and human capital.

When I recruit, my experience as an owner enables me to fully understand the importance of having the right people in the right positions. That experience informs my decisions and makes a huge difference for the teams I work with, and their bottom lines. Many of our clients and their team members indicate that working within the flow of their profiles has taken the "work" out of business. The benefits of working in flow are many. Staff turnover and sick leave are reduced and KSIs and financial targets are being exceeded, even during these tougher economic times. Essentially, dynamic teams are being created; they're achieving high levels of success and loving the experience!

Natural alignment creates a totally new experience and an atmosphere of grace and ease. Professionally, all I do is create, and I'm ecstatic. It was huge to learn that daily management is not my value in an organization, and to do that now would be disempowering and exhausting. Client assessment, product testing, devising expansion strategies — I love doing that! And at Wealth Recruitment Strategies, we've done our market research, tested the product and are flying. When you're working with people who resonate with your vision and are in profile, it's amazing what can be accomplished in a short time.

But it's not just about my business. It's about my life, my whole life. My husband did his profile and learned that he is a Lord. Because I know this, I understand his reactions when we're assessing my ongoing and increasing list of business ideas. I also understand the many differences in how we see the world. Understanding our profiles certainly gives us each a new level of appreciation for the other's points of view.

Natural alignment creates a totally new experience and an atmosphere of grace and ease.

There is no comparison between my life before and after Wealth Dynamics — business and life are so very different! It's this experience of deep change, and empowerment to be in flow, that I share with other entrepreneurs and managers. In these challenging economic times, operating a business according to one's profile is imperative. In playing your natural game and building dynamic teams to support your vision, you strengthen your foundation for success. More importantly, you find an inherent joy in your work. What could be more important than that?

Helen Bichel, founder of Wealth Recruitment Strategies, has over fifteen years' experience as a recruitment specialist and business consultant. Helen has broad business experience in organizational visioning, business strategy, development, planning and leveraging. A key element to her success has been her ability to innovate and provide cutting-edge solutions for processes and organizational management. She continues to generate innovative solutions to the recruitment process through working with team development for medium-sized enterprises in Australia.

Her greatest passion is seeing people excel in their personal lives and at work. To learn more about Helen, her company and her services, please visit www.WealthRecruitment Strategies.com

The Great Orchestra: Chemistry at Work

NIKKI SLADE

Over the centuries, it's been said that in this life, we are all instruments in one great orchestra. Our greatest challenge and reward lies in finding our parts and playing in tune. This is often easier said than done, and yet, when we get it right, everything changes, personally and professionally.

The power of sound enables us to attune to our true inner creative potential. As we tap into this, we begin to resonate in harmony with ourselves and others. We experience being a team player on a deeper level and then become naturally in harmony with the ensemble to which we belong. At this moment we are highly energized; our relatedness with others increases and a sense of joy is achieved in creating and producing effective results at work. When this harmony arises there is freedom and ease in all tasks. Work naturally turns into play! This brings greater enthusiasm, passion and purpose into all areas of our lives, from family to the corporate environment. It all comes down to expressing who we truly are.

My passion is to provide an uplifting space where clients liberate their creative expression, and fulfill their promises from a place of authenticity and joy. When focused on directed outcomes, voice-work produces dramatic effects on a personal and a professional level. Teams I've worked with in this way have reported a huge shift in enthusiasm and an unleashing of creative ideas previously hidden from view. In this glorious space, opportunities show up, breakthroughs occur and relationships open and deepen.

Voice-work achieves such magical results. Primordial sound is a powerful key to positive transformation with teams and individuals. These ancient sounds are deeply inspiring, heart-opening and calming; they replenish the soul. Core sound work clears the mind and gives us greater clarity to focus on delivering effective results. It helps each of us to get in touch with our true flow, which is where we excel. When we feel heard and fully empowered, we naturally play together with freedom and ease as one united orchestra.

The focus of the work is a mutual participation, rather than a performance, so that the pressure is off the individual and toward the collective nature of the experience. Teams have often been amazed at how rapidly barriers have come down with one other. The more voices that come together, the more rewarding the outcome will be. When a group unites in the power of sound, each member resonating her 'true note,' a certain magical chemistry occurs that creates a whole greater than the parts. Getting this attunement right is invaluable – that's why businesses consistently invest so heavily in team building.

Voice-work achieves such magical results.

Once, for example, I was asked to do a conference for a big chocolate company in Europe. The organizers asked me to get everyone into an energized, fun space during the break so that they'd be alert and present during a long series of presentations through the rest of the morning and the afternoon. There were a lot of women there, so I got them all singing along to Sister Sledge's "We Are Family." Once the ice was broken, their receptivity was palpable. Halfway through the break I was leading them in a universal chant from the heart, which this group of stoic Northerners would never in their lives have done before! They were surprised at how moved and open they had become. For the rest of the day, the group was in flow, riding the wave and trusting where it took them. And when complete trust is present, absolute magic happens! Apparently, the group continued singing well into the evening.

Contrast this with the 'average' corporate conference. How memorable do employees typically find them, and how long lasting are the returns for the business?

A harmonious, in-flow venture will involve the specific skills and personalities of many different profiles, just as a solid orchestra will have all its sections and instruments working together to make beautiful music.

In more recent months, I have thoroughly enjoyed incorporating Wealth Dynamics into my work, helping clients to resonate fully with their natural profiles. I've seen this work powerfully with large groups, private clients and my own business.

The more voices that come together,
the more rewarding the outcome will be.

Wealth Dynamics has enabled me to create a more successful voice-work business. Beforehand, I had never been aware of how many key players I was missing in the orchestra of my own professional life. One month I would have a surge in business, and the next would see a dip. Through my Star profile, I've come to one of my most important epiphanies: I am the worst person to run my business! This home truth has brought me new and greater momentum than I've ever experienced before.

My job as a Star profile is to shine a light on my vision for sharing my voice-work globally. For a long time, I managed and promoted my business, and did the bookkeeping, and I struggled to fulfill these roles easily. But then I met a Trader, a Lord and another Star, each of whom has brought invaluable depth to the team. Lindsey and Hanna were great fans of my work, coming to every event and voice-work session. It was obvious for a while that they both were wonderfully in flow with me and my business, deeply invested in pursuing their own authentic voice-work and in contributing to its growth and presence in the world. Then suddenly, one day, I understood that they were just the people I needed on my team.

Looking at Lindsey and Hanna's Wealth Dynamics profiles, we determined what their best, specific roles in the company should be. Lindsey is a Trader, with a phenomenal ability to care for my existing clients and keep them coming back for more. As a Star, I was hopeless at that. Though they would have returned, I didn't know how to invite them. Thanks to Trader Lindsey, the size of my groups has tripled. Hanna, another Star, is fantastic with PR. I shine a light on my work and my mission, and she uses her Star power to shine a light on me. Because of her abilities, our recent "Be Your Own Valentine" event was sold out — with a waiting list!

And Kay, a Lord who came on board a little later, is an absolute Godsend. I no longer have to waste my energy or dam up my flow, trying to deal with minutiae, or more importantly, manage the financial performance of my business. As a Lord, Kay adores handling the details and profitability, and nothing slips past her eagle eye.

Using Wealth Dynamics, I have created a team that has brought incredible life and professional fulfillment my way. We all operate from a Wealth Dynamics perspective, so we communicate and work brilliantly together. We have a lot of fun, too. For the first time, I have a full orchestra, with a fabulous chemistry that makes great music together. It's like having a business family.

A harmonious, in-flow venture will involve the specific skills and personalities of many different profiles, just as a solid orchestra will have all its sections and instruments working together to make beautiful music.

With this fantastic team behind my work, and with our new collective experience of Wealth Dynamics in action, we realized that countless group ventures were sorely in need of these resources. That's when we developed Chemistry at Work, a specialized coaching process that synthesizes the principles of Wealth Dynamics and my work with sound and voice, to create harmonious, vibrant and effective businesses. Through this process corporations are able to foster true relatedness in teams, align powerfully in the face of conflicting ideas, and become highly effective and efficient in realizing company vision.

What if one day, everyone came together with one sound, one voice and one heart? How would the corporate world be different if people were fully able to express their creative potential? How would your business — your world be different, if all beings worked together harmoniously? It is in that world that all you envision for your business is not only possible, it is inevitable.

Nikki Slade's successful early career as an actress and singer prepared her to work with audiences and groups of every size and variety. She has pioneered voice and sound work in the UK for over eighteen years, offering voice-work sessions to a wide range of individuals, and groups including Deutsche Bank, addicts at the Priory Hospital, inmates at Wandsworth Prison and account holders at MC Saatchi.

Nikki Slade Chemistry at Work propels businesses and organizations into highly increased states of efficiency, harmony, creativity and shared goal and vision fulfillment. Her unique services include creative juice sessions, conference ice-breakers, team building and vision creation groups, residential retreats and private voice work. For further details, see www.NikkiSlade.com.

Letting Go, Making Peace

SUSAN PAUL

There's a powerful image, a metaphor that has influenced me deeply ever since Roger Hamilton evoked it during his "Your Life, Your Legacy" conference that I attended with my husband some years ago. To explain the way most of us live our lives, Roger painted this picture: You're in a stream. You're in a stream — but instead of letting go and flowing with the natural movement of the water, you're clinging desperately to a rock, hanging on for dear life. Hearing this, my husband turned to me, laughing. "I wonder what your rock is?" I teased back, "Don't even go there. I've worked too long and hard to let go of anything, let alone my rock." "I give you three months," he replied. "By then I want you to have left the law. It's time for you to play a bigger game."

My rock was my career — being a judge. After seventeen years as a lawyer, the last five years of which I had been a judge, I thought I'd reached the pinnacle of my profession. Having a successful career had always been very important to me, especially coming from a poor and Asian background. But somehow, in spite of all my achievements, I never thoroughly believed in what I did for a living. I loved certain aspects of it, but the law always felt stifling to me on some level. I don't ever recall waking up in the morning and thinking, "I can't wait to get to court today!"

In many ways my profession simply did not suit my nature. Though I was a lawyer, I was forever trying to find solutions for my clients to make sure they never had to go anywhere near a courtroom. I wanted them to find win-win solutions that worked for them on every level. So, when I found out, using Wealth Dynamics profiling, that I was a Creator, my frustrations with the pre-scriptive legal process finally made sense. As a Creator I am naturally innovative, can see the bigger picture and love finding new ways to solve problems.

Creativity, however, is not allowed in the judicial process. I doubt I would have lasted very long as a judge if I had followed my natural instincts and sim-ply stopped hearings to insist that both sides talk to each other. I can't tell you how often I found myself sitting in a hearing, thinking, "If only you had spent your time, money and energy really communicating with each other, instead of having a verbal fistfight through your lawyers, you might have discovered the underlying issues here, created a solution that actually works for you, that did not cost so much and might even increase the profitability of your organiza-tion!" Of course, as a judge, I couldn't give voice to those thoughts. I simply did my job, which was to look at the facts and make sound and fair judgments according to the law at that time.

My rock was my career — being a judge.

So, until I encountered Wealth Dynamics, a tension existed between my personal identification with my career in the law as a judge — my rock — and my true calling as a mediator and facilitator of extraordinary leadership within organizations and communities. On the second day of Roger's conference I thought to myself, "What if? What if I could actually make a difference on a larger scale?" I was already a qualified mediator, but I knew that until I com-mitted to a future in mediation, I would always be torn between two different ways of working. My creativity would continue to be stifled as a judge and I would not be in flow.

The solution was obvious. I retired from my position as judge; I let go of the rock. To say the least, my boss was shocked. To be honest, I was also shocked. I had worked so hard to get to that position. But in the end it was such a relief to simply let go and make space for potentially great things to happen. And I don't regret my decision for one minute. I love that I now get to assist my clients in creating innovative and workable solutions to their disputes and to lead their businesses to greater success by building powerful relationships. My experience with employment issues in the courtroom reinforced my belief that effective leadership is the key to harmony in any group, whether in the family, the workplace or among a community of nations.

If you look at the family unit, for example, you can see what makes it functional (or not). If parents are providing leadership through stability, focus and agreed standards of behavior, the whole family feels a sense of certainty — and therefore a level of security, no matter the family's external circumstances. When children know what is and is not acceptable, they have a secure space in which to develop and grow. That makes for a stronger and more fulfilled family unit in which all members get to be themselves.

If nobody takes leadership within a family, if no one articulates boundaries and goals, discord is created and that safe space for development and harmony is lost. The same holds true for organizations, which are a reflection of their leadership. A successful organization, like a functional family, begins with its leaders being in flow, crystal clear about what they stand for. A leader who is in flow with both her natural game and the vision for her organization can effortlessly inspire and support absolutely everyone on her team.

My experience with employment issues in the courtroom reinforced my belief that effective leadership is the key to harmony in any group, whether in the family, the workplace or among a community of nations.

This internal harmony and respect spreads outward to the organization's customers, clients, vendors, partner organizations — everyone. It has a ripple effect. If people are happy at work, they'll bring that joy home to ripple through the family. And vice versa. This is the kind of dynamic that fosters powerful relationships between employees and employers, spouses and children, and even between parties who might otherwise fight it out in the courtroom. I'm convinced that it can also bring peace on a global scale.

Much has happened since I let go of my rock. I've formed an innovative me-diation consultancy called Eternal Alliances. Our message is simple: "Innovate: Mediate: Communicate." We have created a harmonious and well-rounded team with the strengths of a Supporter and an Accumulator to draw on, as well as my own Creator energies, which are always joyfully at work creating projects to fulfill our vision. Recognizing my value as a Creator, I've let go of doing ev-erything to make room for the skills and passions of my colleagues, who handle numbers and other aspects of the business better than I ever could. Because we each understand our roles and are in flow, pursuing our common vision, we impart that effectiveness to every organization and community we assist.

Eternal Alliances has pioneered a holistic approach to mediation, believing that this has been missing for many of our clients' organizations and commu-nities, and that it will form the cornerstone of their future success and wealth creation. If we consult from a perspective that creates room for each employee to feel valued and respected, we're pursuing our goal of promoting peace and tolerance in the world, person by person, organization by organization, com-munity by community. And the ripple effect moves ever outward.

Because we each understand our roles and are in flow, pursuing our common vision, we impart that effectiveness to every organization and community we assist.

Effective leadership moves from the top down, but that does not mean those furthest from the top don't count, or benefit less: quite the contrary. Instead, each team member contributes his natural passions and talents, in flow. And management recognizes each team member may have dreams and aspirations outside of the common setting that also deserve respect and support. The goal is not how to extract the maximum from each other, but how to help each person find true flow and fulfill his vision.

If someone is in a role or job that is off-profile, she is probably clinging to her own personal rock — and may not even recognize it! I didn't recognize mine. She is probably frustrated and taking that out into the world. The beauty of following the Wealth Dynamics model is that instead of being frustrated, or even vaguely dissatisfied with life, she could be inspired by the direction her life is going in and what she is achieving. That will spill over into a desire to help others feel the same way. A skilled leader will notice and facilitate change that helps her colleagues let go of "their rock" and enjoy the flow of the stream.

So, my question for you is: What role, what idea, what "rock" are you clinging to? What could it mean to you — your family — your business — your organization — your community — if you simply let go?

Susan Paul, a CEDR accredited mediator, Wealth Dynamics Master Practitioner and specialist in leadership development and alternative dispute resolution, is CEO of Eternal Alliances. Her personal commitment is to promote extraordinary leadership, wealth creation and peace through the creation of powerful relationships within organizations and communities. Susan has over twenty years experience as a UK General Commercial Lawyer and over eighteen years experience as a Specialist UK Employment Lawyer. Most recently, she was an Employment Judge for the Ministry of Justice in London for five years. She is also the managing partner of E12 Health, a general medical practice serving ten thousand patients in East London. Now retired from the judiciary, Susan has continued to the next stage of her varied business career through Eternal Alliances to become a social entrepreneur. To learn more about Susan visit www.EternalAlliances.com.

Ask Better Questions

MARTYN ANSTEY

It seemed we might have to dig forever. After Hurricane Stan blew through Guatemala, one of the villages had been completely wiped out by mudslides. We were digging for remains. More than fifteen hundred people had died in one night. In the neighboring villages thousands more were left homeless. My shovel hit something hard — the roof of someone's house, or a car. Looking around, I noticed everyone was digging, but everyone was also hungry and thirsty. Many were hurt and most had lost everything. I thought, "I'm digging because they asked me to dig because they need *someone* to dig. But what do they really need and how can I provide the solution?"

I realized I could make a bigger difference. I put down my shovel and got to work doing what I do best: shining a light on a dream, a proven concept or, in this case, a crisis. The dreams of the Guatemalan people were basic and urgent: shelter, food, clean water, medical assistance and supplies. Just as I had raised the profile of major brands in my career, I worked to draw attention to the crisis in Guatemala by organizing an event. I also built a network around the event and inspired international companies to donate products. The result was a successful fundraising event that attracted media attention and more money, food and medical equipment.

But what would have happened if I had continued to dig? I may have found a body to bury, but ultimately the survivors would have struggled to go on with less of everything. I was able to produce real results because I asked a better question and stuck to my core competencies. Your dreams may not be as basic or as urgent as the needs of the villagers, but they are vital to you. How could you improve your outcomes if you stopped what you're doing now and asked a better question? What results could you produce if you focused on what you do best?

What will happen to your dreams if YOU keep "digging?" Sometimes you have to stop doing what's expected of you and regroup. You have to "go to the balcony" and give yourself critical thinking time. I do this often, and I begin by focusing on my vision and then I brainstorm how to live it in my everyday life. But I haven't always approached life or business in this way.

When I started out in business, I set a goal of running a large company, one with at least five hundred employees. At the time, this seemed a good measure of success. My first job after graduation was in Kimberly Clark's Graduate Brand Management Program, where I helped launch international brands such as Huggies® and Kleenex®. I was successful in part because I put myself in the target audience's shoes. I was able to come up with a solution for their problems that they would be willing to pay for.

What will happen to your dreams if YOU keep "digging?"

When Pearson recruited me to join the team charged with taking The Financial Times Group (FT Group) brand global, I was thrilled. For nearly five years I launched FT Group brands globally across Europe, the Americas, Africa, the Middle East and the Asian Pacific. As Head of Channel Marketing EMEA, my position was more about developing profitable marketing and commercial systems than advertising/promotions. I enjoyed shaking things up at the FT Group, developing new streams of revenue by expanding the company into new markets, new sectors and new product offerings. But I wasn't truly fulfilled. I enjoyed bringing people together on a project, but I didn't love the everyday stuff. I wanted to be great at it — to be great at everything — but I just wasn't.

So I decided to make a radical change. I had always wanted to volunteer, but kept putting it off in favor of accepting new job promotions and exciting projects. To some, it seemed like a crazy move to give up my amazing job. But that's exactly what I did. I knew from the moment I drafted my resignation letter that I had made the right decision. I planned a three-month sabbatical to help in youth development projects in remote villages in Nicaragua. When I saw all the work that had to be done, I stayed on. For two years I volunteered across Latin America. It was during this time that I helped the hurricane relief efforts in Guatemala. I imagined a life of travel and volunteerism, but I was frustrated with how some charitable organizations focused their energies. I realized I could make a huge difference by not only drawing upon my business and entrepreneurial skills, but also by leveraging my wide network.

Then I became ill. The medical bills were large and nearly wiped out my cash reserves. So I returned to the workforce as General Manager for an educational company, Wall Street Institute. I was charged with the goal of increasing the company's valuation for a trade sale to a private equity company. We achieved this objective by launching into new segments, new markets and leveraging networks through strategic alliances. This experience gave me my first clue that my purpose was to increase value, rather than manage a team. In my next position, Head of Marketing Asia Pacific for National Geographic Channels and Fox International, I went from managing two hundred people to managing ten people, and I realized it was more important for me to create strategic value, rather than manage a team.

I also use Wealth Dynamics for companies. When I create the framework for a project, I evaluate each company and assign it a Wealth Dynamics profile. One company may be the Creator, one company may be the Star, one company may be the Trader or Deal Maker, all working together, doing what they do best.

Later, when I encountered Wealth Dynamics, I realized I was on the right track. I don't have to be perfect in everything. I have a core skill, and I should be focusing on that. Brilliant! Wealth Dynamics gave me the ability to let go of things. I no longer expect to be the greatest at everything. Sometimes when you focus on the things you're not naturally amazing at, you end up with a grade

D. And then when you focus on the things you are naturally amazing at, you get an A. Which means your life averages out as a B or a C.

Do you really want to live an average life? I don't. I live a grade-A life, in part because I focus on my core competencies. Now, I no longer have the egocentric goal of managing five hundred people. In fact, now I love to work with a small core team! I'm all about minimizing risk and increasing my return on Time, Investment, and Peace of mind — what I call a Return on TIP.

In the past, I made mistakes because I took on roles that didn't suit me. I no longer feel the need to be the creator of everything. As a Star profile, I know my job is not to recreate the wheel, or start the process. My role is to shine a light on a project, company or organization and help expand its potential.

You don't have to be perfect at everything. Determine the path that's right for you, even if everyone else thinks you should be doing something else.

When I founded my company, marketOXYGEN, I assembled a dream team of proven industry winners. We partner with people who have big vision and big plans to start up, launch, expand, or turn around their companies. I ask potential partners to take a Wealth Dynamics profile test, and from that I am able to see how we will all work together toward a common objective. Not everyone has the same game. By employing Wealth Dynamics, I'm able to "go to the balcony" and figure out how to move pieces, how to link companies together, how to leverage the skills of all involved and produce amazing results. I also use Wealth Dynamics for companies. When I create the framework for a project, I evaluate each company and assign it a Wealth Dynamics profile. One company may be the Creator, one company may be the Star, one company may be the Trader or Deal Maker, all working together, doing what they do best.

This is how I finally realized my vision for giving back. I could volunteer for the rest of my life, but I would never make the difference we are making now through for-profit social enterprise. Some companies are great at raising money. Some companies are committed to donating. Other companies are fantastic at getting media attention. Rather than focus on how each company could improve its own efforts, I asked a better question: how can we work together to change the world? Through my large network, I link people, and all of a sudden we have companies in flow, working toward the common good.

You don't have to be perfect at everything. Determine the path that's right for you, even if everyone else thinks you should be doing something else. Even if you think you should be doing something else.

As my great friend and mentor John Booth says, "Be generous, be outstanding, be grateful." You can choose to dig, to keep at something even when you might know a better way, or have more to offer. Or you can put down the shovel and ask your first better question: "How could I make a bigger difference — in my career, my business, my family, my community, my life — by doing what comes naturally?"

Martyn Anstey is the founder of marketOXYGEN, a company on a mission to transform the planet by helping launch and grow companies through effective business, sales and marketing strategies and systems that work in the real world. In addition to gaining access to capital, clients receive investment advisory services to maximize company valuations, but most importantly, access to a world-class team of people who have been there, done it and succeeded.

Martyn holds a First Class BSc Honors Degree in business and management studies, as well as other management diplomas and certificates. He is the recipient of the IBM Student of the Year Award, and placed second of more than four hundred teams in the Institute of Direct Marketing (IDM) Awards. A veteran of marketing and business development for global brands, Martyn has held positions with brands such as Huggies®, Kleenex®, Andrex, The Financial Times Group, National Geographic, MarketWatch.com, Wall Street Institute, Fox International and Citroen. Learn more about Martyn's work at www.LaunchCatalyst.com.at and www.marketOXYGEN.com.

The Self-Esteem Queen

RAEWYN WELLER

Once my children were old enough to go to school, I felt a strong urge to get out into the world and start doing things. So I acted on that urge, and had my hands in so many pies. I created and ran successful businesses; I continued to be an involved parent; I was a district councilor; I volunteered to organize various festivals and activities, commercial and civic — you name it, I did it.

For several years, I organized the local annual Kiwifruit Festival, which is unique to Te Puke, New Zealand, the kiwifruit capital of the World. Part of my job was to put on the End-of-Festival Ball and Kiwifruit Queen Contest. I had hired someone to emcee, but as I watched the contest from the wings, I felt a keen longing to be the emcee myself. I had wanted to do it even before I hired someone else, but I'd felt I wasn't good enough. For me, watching that contest was almost painful. I missed out on a great deal in life simply because I lacked confidence. And what's even sadder, it wasn't a lack of confidence about things I wasn't able to do. I lacked confidence to go ahead and do precisely those things that I really *wanted* to be doing; things I was meant to do, all along. The problem was, I was a victim of my own negative thinking. As much as I wanted to be on that stage, I was the one keeping me from getting up there. I was the one putting myself down.

There's a phenomenon in New Zealand we call "The Tall Poppy Syndrome." Basically, it means that when one person starts to shine, starts to rise taller than the others, those others find a way to pull that tall one down, to chop off its head. Twenty years ago, when it wasn't yet common for women to be leaders, I always was. I was ahead of my time, constantly in the public eye. Nobody tore me down or chopped off my head — but they didn't have to. I lacked confidence to the degree that I chopped my own head off. I created my own Tall Poppy Syndrome.

In the 1930s, Dr. Thurman Fleet developed "The Stickman Concept." A lot of people in business are applying the concept now, most notably Bob Proctor. Symbolized by the drawing of a stickman with a huge head, representing the mind, the concept argues that your mind manifests the results of your life; that is, your body and your actions are just manifestations of what's going on in your mind. Put another way, whenever I'm hosting one of my seminars or workshops, I like to tell people that we can change the results of our lives by changing how we think.

So the reason I was not up on that stage emceeing was simply that I didn't think it was my place to be up on that stage emceeing, even though it's what I desperately wanted to do. Now I'm onstage all the time. What changed my thinking, and therefore changed me, was Wealth Dynamics.

Put another way, whenever I'm hosting one of my seminars or workshops, I like to tell people that we can change the results of our lives by changing how we think.

My whole life I suspected I was a Star, even though I didn't know that was the term for who I was. Doing my Wealth Dynamics profile and learning I was a Star was a real revelation for me. It validated everything I had been feeling my entire life. It confirmed every suspicion I'd had about myself. And most importantly, learning I was a Star gave me immediate confidence to go out and do all those things I'd been wanting to do for so long, things I now knew I was supposed to be doing. The first time I got on stage after learning my profile, I did a presentation of a workshop I'd put together based on Roger Hamilton's book, Wink. My audience was XL people, who immediately validated that I am a Star and belong onstage, in front of others. Just to further test my new awareness, though, I went to Toastmasters to hone my public speaking skills. After speaking I was asked what I was doing there, since I was so natural at it!

The experience I had as a result of learning my profile was so profound that I realized I wanted to do it for others. So I opened my own business, Wealth In Knowledge, dedicated to helping others grow in all aspects of their lives. My purpose, my mission and my business are to empower others to live the lives they deserve — and to be a "Life Success GPS" that guides people on the path to success, helping them change their results by helping them change the way they think. My workshops are a holistic experience, because when we talk about wealth, we're talking about all areas of our lives. But it all starts with a Wealth Dynamics profile, because if you don't know your profile, you don't know what it is you're supposed to be doing. And if you're not doing what you where born to do, what you are passionate about, chances are very good that you're not particularly happy.

I have noticed an undeniable link: people who do their Wealth Dynamics profiles emerge more confident. In some cases, such as mine, it's instant; in others it takes a little more time. The key is acceptance. Once you accept the verdict of your profile, you surge with a newfound self-confidence.

Too many people stay in certain jobs far too long, not because they love them but simply because they're good at them. Competence is important, but if you don't feel passion for what you're doing, you'll never be happy doing it, no matter how good you are at it. In my workshops, we use a graph that measures both competence and passion.

It's not only about knowing your profile, though; it's also about accepting it. I have worked with a couple of Deal Makers who frankly didn't want to be Deal Makers. When they first learned their profiles, they were in disbelief. But then when they looked more closely at their pasts and slowly realized they were, in fact, Deal Makers (and good ones to boot), they became reconciled to the idea, even pleased. I have noticed an undeniable link: people who do their Wealth Dynamics profiles emerge more confident. In some cases, such as mine, it's instant; in others it takes a little more time. The key is acceptance. Once you accept the verdict of your profile, you surge with a newfound self-confidence.

It's one thing to know what you are, but it's quite another to take action to move into the place you deserve to be. A current client of mine is a lady who found out she's a Star but is still working in a CPA's office. She's miserable, but she is in a comfort zone. So I'm working with her to get her to take some necessary action, something she's more inclined to do now that she's more confident in herself.

> *One cannot change people; they have to change themselves. One can only plant the seeds in peoples' minds in order to get them to realize their competence and passions by themselves.*

And of course, knowing your profile is fundamental in knowing your true path in the first place. I'm employing people to do what I'm not happy doing, those tasks that I had become competent at but lacked any real passion to do. But it also works the other way around: that is, some people do jobs they have a passion for but no competence in. I had a client who's a Mechanic, but he wanted to do presentations and be a Star. Just because people have knowledge about a product and even passion for it, doesn't mean they have the competence to get it across and sell it in the way a Star does. So I worked with this person to help him realize that he can earn more money by working with a Star and continuing to do what he does best as a Mechanic.

One cannot change people; they have to change themselves. One can only plant the seeds in peoples' minds in order to get them to realize their competence and passions by themselves.

Another way Wealth Dynamics can be really helpful is that if you know your own profile and understand the parameters of other profiles, you can read other people better. This is a great asset as an employer. Once you get a sense of a person as an introvert or extrovert, you can start asking better, more specific questions regarding that person's skills, establishing a great sense of where to place him or her in your business.

Reading others is also useful when it comes to networking. In my workshops, we talk about many different ways you can network, many effective ways to communicate with a variety of people; but to be able to do any of that, you have to be able to identify, on the spot, who other people are and how they think. That identification process is strongly enhanced by knowledge of Wealth Dynamics.

I love sharing. I love seeing people have their own "Aha!" moments, and realize their own potential. Helping others is a win-win situation; it helps both my clients and myself to grow and feel fulfilled. Recently, at a local Chamber of Commerce meeting, I clicked onto a phrase that felt like it described me perfectly: "the Self-Esteem Queen." The idea had never really struck me before, but once it hit, it stuck, because I realized that that's what I do. When people come to see me, they get their self-esteem lifted.

It's all about attitude, about confidence. Wealth Dynamics helped me to find my confidence, and I love helping others find theirs. My name, Raewyn, outside of New Zealand or Australia, is an unusual name. So whenever I'm at a conference, I always tell people, "Just think of a ray of sunshine and a winner, and you'll remember my name." That's how I like to think of myself: a ray of sunshine that helps others to become winners — thereby becoming a winner myself.

Raewyn Weller is founder and director of Wealth in Knowledge, a business dedicated to helping people to change and grow in all aspects of their lives. She is the author of the inspirational book Jan's Dash, a biography integrated with personal development. She has managed and/or owned several businesses, and has held government appointments in business and immigration. Raewyn is a Certified Life Success Consultant, a Justice of the Peace, a marriage celebrant and a personal development coach and speaker. To learn more about Raewyn, visit www.WealthinKnowledge.com and www.jansdash.co.nz.

From Suffering
to Heartfelt Joy

SAMANTHA KELLY

In my twenty years of work as a Registered Nurse, I've seen that most people are suffering greatly. It may be surprising that, given my background, it is not physical pain I see people suffering from the most; rather, the greatest pain seems to come when people find that their human potentials have gone unrealized. Orthodox medicine does not usually acknowledge the connection between illness and the unlived life.

The bulk of my nursing work has been with those dying — at home and in hospital and hospice settings — helping them during their end-of-life journeys. My other focus is on imprisoned people. You might not automatically detect a similarity between these groups; but in both, the pain of unrealized potential seems to be the greatest obstacle to transcendence, self-acceptance and joy. When someone holds on tightly at the end of his life, there is incompletion. If he hasn't been an active part of creating and designing his life, he won't be ready to let it go when the time comes. When you're facing imminent death, all of your unfinished business and unresolved conflicts come up. Suffering at the end of life is primarily a result of denying these parts of self. If a client is struggling in this way, I offer support to help her give up attachment to what could have been and control over what will happen. In this last chapter of her story, opportunity for change lies entirely within her mindset.

That's also true for my clients in prisons. Crime is often created as part of a system of pain, repression and self-limiting beliefs. Most of the people I work with have experienced abuse and struggle with pain-anesthetizing addictions. They were never supported or acknowledged for the beauty of who they are; nor can they see that their lives are their own — potentially joyful — creations.

For all of us, no matter our circumstances and achievements, the real prison is the prison of the mind.

Sometimes it takes only the discovery of a single key to open the prison doors; sometimes it is as simple as helping someone to become aware of the goodness within. It has become my passion and my life's work to help those in prison and anyone else willing to break free from the prisons the mind has created, to transform suffering to heartfelt joy — leading to vibrant health. I deliver a message of hope to those seeking opportunity through pain, possibility through despair.

For all of us, no matter our circumstances and achievements, the real prison is the prison of the mind.

Before I discovered Wealth Dynamics, though, I was just as much in prison as the people I work with. I enjoyed my work as a nurse, but I was living a life of mediocrity, unfulfilled through self-limiting beliefs; I was putting off following my true path. Like so many people, I didn't really see myself as separate from the identity others had created for me through their own agenda and expectations. (Many don't look at that; or, if they do, feel helpless to act.) I was still playing a role invented for me by others.

I was also conditioned to live my life independently, not wishing to be reliant on others or indebted to their generosity. Being beholden to someone else, I might have to sacrifice my own dreams to fulfill a repayment. Eventually, however, I realized that I needed support for my true expression. I needed to accept contribution from others in order to live my passion of doing transformative work with people who are imprisoned by society or by their own minds.

I'd thought that my vision for integrated health was a little too edgy for most of mainstream society and its fragmentary approach to illness. But between my own growing self-awareness and the enthusiastic acknowledgement of my profile by my XL associates, I began to see that it was just the right time for me to speak up. I am a Star, and my greatest value lies in my ability to take powerful messages to diverse groups, connecting deeply and very quickly with people from all walks of life.

When I feel strongly about something, my message is delivered straight from my heart to the hearts of others, inspiring and empowering them. I make that message relevant to others' experience, and I feel I am being guided by a source greater than myself. My biggest lesson is learning to "let go" — and in letting go, my life is falling into place. The less I try, the more easily life flows. Finding this detachment is like opening the prison doors and stepping outside. Life can't flow without it.

In applying the knowledge of my wealth profile, I am learning to trust the process of flow more each day. Like my palliative clients, I am giving up control in order to open to the discovery of who I am and where my true path is leading me. These days, I say "yes" a great deal more often than I say "no." Each experience, even if I would never repeat it, provides more clarity and focus about how I can go about creating the kind of life that truly represents my authentic self. To attract butterflies without a net, say yes!

The less I try, the more easily life flows. Finding this detachment is like opening the prison doors and stepping outside. Life can't flow without it.

Dynamo energy is about making the rules as you go through a journey of exploration. Blaze energy is about human connection, delivering a message. In recognizing these influences, I have been able to gain a broader perspective of what fits and what doesn't. The more versatile and creative you are in exploring your true nature, the more life will bring opportunities that resonate with your truth.

I seek to give meaning to my ambition. Why do I do what I do? Because, when I witness suffering, I want to help alleviate it. I want to serve by helping people move from suffering to heartfelt joy. My community validates and supports that desire, helping it to flow. In essence, my values and my ambition are one and the same. I believe that's the core we all need to hold onto for wealth attraction — not ego. And it keeps my hope alive without my even trying. A message of hope is the essential ingredient to those feeling trapped within the confines of their current circumstances. When I've asked questions of my clients in the prison about their life purpose, their contributions and what kind of legacy they want to leave behind for future generations, I've seen that the mere suggestion of another perspective, and the opportunity to tell their stories and give voice to their dreams, has transformed great pain and despair into excitement and a sense of possibility.

I'm so passionate about this work that I love to speak about it. And when I speak about it, others are moved by the deep resonance of connection we all seek. They feel genuine excitement about the project. They want to be involved.

Wealth Dynamics principles are a natural fit for my work with imprisoned people. In determining profile, a person discovers a whole set of specific strategies and tools to help appreciate natural gifts and wonderful attributes — and break free from habitual, self-sabotaging thinking and behavior. What has been lacking, up until now, is the presence of adequate role models to introduce these possibilities for healing and finding truth.

Wealth Dynamics has shown me that, as a Star, it is my calling to help create a context for growth for these people I care about and believe in. I leverage my profile to share stories and show them concrete examples of how living a life in flow can bring freedom — a valuable model to help lead them into the future.

I'm so passionate about this work that I love to speak about it. And when I speak about it, others are moved by the deep resonance of connection we all seek. They feel genuine excitement about the project. They want to be involved. My team is growing, and creating a variety of programs to offer support for imprisoned people in the development of their self-esteem and self-awareness.

Now, what seemed like a distant dream for them is evolving into a realistic future. They are transmuting, transforming their suffering into heartfelt joy.

Samantha Kelly has worked in the UK and Canada as a Registered Nurse since 1990, discovering along the way that mainstream health services are reactive to physical symptoms and therefore unlikely to alleviate disease, which is subject to influences of the mind and emotion. Recent work within prisons for men and women has again highlighted to Samantha how paralyzed we become by the limitation of our beliefs.

Inspired by those in prison, Samantha discovered the opportunity to walk into the places that cause discomfort. It is therefore no surprise that she has become a facilitator for the organization, "Be the Change" (www.BeTheChange.com), promoting the work of "The Pachamama Alliance" (www.AwakeningTheDreamer.org), and, together with her enthusiasm to bring integrated medicine into the mainstream, supporting the work of Dr. Rosy Daniel and "Health Creation" (www.HealthCreation.co.uk). Samantha brings her wisdom through training in answering the question, "How do we live, knowing that one day we will die?" Visit reconnectinghumanity.blogspot.com.

Turning Meaning Into Profit

MATTHEW NEWNHAM

All marketers tell a story. The "this is the best price and value" story is just one of those available, and in fact, it's rarely the most effective for the audience you may be trying to reach.

— Seth Godin

Early one morning in Seattle, we waited hopefully for the fish-throwing to start. We were on a family holiday, and had stopped at the world-famous Pike Place Fish Market. As we admired the stunning display of fish and seafood, my wife and I explained to our two sons how the fishmongers throw salmon to each other and clown around, drawing large crowds.

It was early morning and business was quiet, so it looked as though we wouldn't see a show this time. Just then, a couple arrived and said they'd like to buy a salmon. The young woman also asked if they could watch their fish being thrown to the man behind the counter. "Absolutely," one of the fishmongers replied. "In fact, why don't you step behind the counter and catch your salmon yourself?" She gasped, gulped and quietly said, "No way, I couldn't catch one of those!"

After some persuading, she made her way behind the counter. As one fishmonger trailed behind, the lady's handbag over his shoulder, another gave her a crash course in fish-catching. A few moments later a large salmon went sailing through the air, over the counter — and, with some subtle assistance, she caught it safely. The lady was relieved, and we were delighted. As the applause faded and we turned to leave, I noticed that the lady's partner had slipped behind the counter to join her. We lingered, sensing something was up. The young man said to his lady, "You might want to look inside the salmon's mouth." She pulled out a small box and opened it to reveal an engagement ring. As her partner went down on bended knee, you could have heard a pin drop. He asked her to marry him and, happily, she said yes. The small crowd applauded again and my wife and I wiped away a few happy tears. (Yes we're incurable romantics, but that day was also our wedding anniversary. Synchronicity is a wonderful thing.)

> *We all agreed that any business could make a difference, if we saw and acted on that possibility.*

Pike Place Fish operates under a simple philosophy: making a difference in their customers' lives, every time they serve them — whether they buy or not. By mastering this philosophy throughout their business, they have become one of the most successful retailers in America — and world famous — with a series of books, DVDs and a training company to show other companies how to create their own version of this type of business. And amazingly, apart from their website, they have never advertised for customers or employees. In fact, they actually have people volunteering to work for them for free.

Pike Place Fish is known for delivering "wow" experiences for their customers. I'm a big fan of this type of business. It's not for everyone, but there are principles you can "borrow" from Pike Place Fish that will enable your business to increase profits, with or without "wow," based on where you are right now.

Roger Hamilton, creator of Wealth Dynamics, says businesses translate meaning into value. In my experience, that's absolutely true. Pike Place Fish took a simple idea — making a difference for each customer — and translated that meaning into unique value for its customers and its team, creating a profitable, sustainable company. Any business can translate its meaning into value to increase profits.

Three simple steps can kick-start this approach in your business. Imagine you sell office supplies. Business doesn't get more ordinary than that, right? In this industry, you might think that all you can compete on is price and service.

After all, that's what everyone else in the industry does. Well, almost everyone. A few years ago, I was giving a presentation on this subject to a group of fellow entrepreneurs in Bali, and I asked if selling one pen or pencil could make an impact. What kind of outcome could be possible? What if one of your pens was used to create a bold new business that became the next Apple or Microsoft? Or what if your pencil inspired a young girl to write stories, and she became the next J. K. Rowling? We all agreed that any business could make a difference, if we saw and acted on that possibility.

> *The real value lies within the outcomes your customers experience and how they feel about those outcomes.*

Within a week of returning home, an amazing coincidence brought this spur-of-the-moment example to life. I learned about a company based here in Scotland called WildHearts in Action, whose founder Mick Jackson is proving that selling office supplies can save lives. Mick nearly died climbing K2, and after being rescued by a little Kashmiri girl, he vowed that business would never be the same for him. WildHearts in Action donates all of its profits to charity, funding essential projects in developing countries. It's able to do this because all WildHearts group companies share a common infrastructure, saving significant costs. But the *reason* it does it at all is because Mick Jackson saw a bigger reason for being in business. This is summed up neatly by the WildHearts tagline, "Even a bad day at the office can save lives."

So step one is to get crystal clear about the meaning behind your business: for you and your family, then for your customers and your team. Achieving this level of clarity is easily one of the most powerful investments you can make in yourself and your business. This critical thinking drives right to the heart of why you're in business, what you're prepared to do to make it work, and how you will connect with others. You can easily spot the difference between those who've done this, and those who haven't. Clarity is a powerful attractor.

Step two is to translate your (renewed) meaning into value for your customers. In simple terms, we know this boils down to explaining the offer to prospects, then delivering it to paying customers. But typically, a lot of meaning gets lost in translation in the journey from concept to words to reality. Isn't it amazing how much effort is expended on convincing prospects to buy and employees to deliver? Why all the struggle? Is it possible that not enough of the original business meaning is being translated effectively into value? The real value lies within the outcomes your customers experience and how they feel about those outcomes.

To start with, how many people do you meet at networking events who answer "What do you do?" with a functional answer, like, "I'm a lawyer." or "I run a marketing company"? Without resorting to hype, isn't it more useful to match our answer authentically to an outcome our ideal prospect really wants? For example, instead of "I'm an online marketer," how about "I help social entrepreneurs increase online sales"?

In the same way, how can our prospects receive full value if we can't attract them with compelling stories to show how we can help — and move them to take action? As veteran marketer John Carlton says, "The marketing landscape is littered with fabulous products that nobody could figure out how to sell." If this isn't your strong suit, how much profit could you recoup by investing in professional help to fix this problem? Of course, telling a compelling story is one thing, but surveys consistently show that most of us have very low expectations as customers, and our actual customer experiences rate even lower! And recent data shows that most employees in the US and Britain are disengaged with their work. That's a huge waste for all concerned. As entrepreneurs, we have a great opportunity to do better on both counts.

Step three is to give your team the same level of meaning that you give your customers, then support them to deliver physically on your business promises. Systems and processes, though vital, can only take a business so far. Ultimately, people run businesses and people deliver profits. And they respond to meaning. What if your business held as much meaning and value for your colleagues as it does for your customers?

We're all familiar with mismatches between what bosses mean and what their teams think they mean. I've spent a large part of my career working with teams to agree on "one version of the truth." But even more seriously, what the business means for founders and executives is usually entirely different from what it means for employees, many of whom often find it difficult to link their roles to meaning and customer value. This is where Wealth Dynamics can really come into its own, helping unite teams via its easily understood common language. I've used it extensively, and I've seen firsthand how productivity and personal fulfillment are boosted dramatically when teams see how each profile creates value, communicates and learns best, and when each member understands their contribution to creating value for customers and the business.

What if your business held as much meaning and value for your colleagues as it does for your customers?

Just seeing the critical difference between your learned behaviors and natural skills can enable you to play fully to each person's strengths, which in itself boosts productivity and morale. Doing this will enable you to connect with your team much more in line with who they *really* are. I've seen this happen many times.

For example, as a Supporter profile, my natural skills are based on working with teams to translate vision into reality. After more than twenty years working on detail-heavy projects, I now know that Accumulator profiles are by nature much stronger as project managers. Can I still manage projects? Yes, but "translator" roles: facilitating, writing and marketing are far more natural for me. Therefore, it makes much more sense to focus my time and energy there instead. We all deliver more value, with greater meaning, when we can operate in roles and teams that allow us to play to our innate skills, talents and passions.

We've looked at how to add *meaning* through rediscovering your personal reasons for doing business, and translating that meaning through effective communication and corresponding actions, to add *value* for your customers and your team. Done well, this approach builds profitable businesses based on *shared meaning.*

This is the real story behind the success of Pike Place Fish. They chose to create a "wow" business that became world famous. Whatever your chosen path, adopting these three steps will create your own level of excellence (even "wow" if you want), where your meaning really does translate to value and profit.

Best wishes on your journey — I'd love to hear how you get on!

Matthew Newnham has spent the past twenty-five years translating meaning into value through communications and business change management. He has helped launch a number of new ventures in both the corporate and entrepreneurial sectors, and he has helped guide organizations through large-scale change at all levels. Matthew's passion has always been the customer offer, and what that means to customers and those who serve them.

More recently, his passion for communicating compelling business stories and offers has led him to focus most of his energies on copywriting and marketing. He is currently supporting the launch and ongoing marketing of several businesses, and is a co-founder of www.Conscious-Wealth.com, which expands in detail on Wealth Dynamics and other successful strategies for personal and business success. Visit www.MeaningIntoProfit. com to learn more about Matthew.

Choosing Better,
Choosing Best

JUDY HAMILTON

Do you look forward to going in to work? Does your job or business make you happy? Does it light you up?

I've made a lot of professional changes in my life, many of them without really realizing what I needed to make me happy. It was only after I did my Wealth Dynamics profile and learned that I was a Deal Maker that I was finally able to make more informed choices, choices I *knew* would lead me to a happier life. And it was only after I learned my profile that so much past unhappiness made sense.

My biggest professional position was at a state art museum. I was Collections Manager (a kind of traffic cop/librarian hybrid), looking after systems and people. I was very good at this and, upon leaving, had an international reputation for excellence in my field. I was so effective at that impersonal sort of management that when I profiled as a Deal Maker, I didn't initially believe it. But I resigned because I was burning out, and I later realized that if the job had been in my natural flow, I wouldn't have been so close to burnout.

Being extremely efficient or competent at something doesn't mean you're in flow. People tend to confuse being proficient at something as being in flow; however, they usually have become proficient over a long period of time, often in incremental steps. It's also the case that people believe they're proficient at something because they've been getting positive feedback from others to this effect. But what they're not factoring in is the energy consumed to gain that proficiency. Acquiring proficiency out of flow means you're really pushing hard to do something that does not come naturally. Then, if you are experiencing burnout or dissatisfaction, you are tempted to blame the level of the workload, a lack of resources or others' inefficiencies in delivering what is required in a timely manner.

But the real problem is that you are not examining if what you're doing is easy, comes naturally or is fun. It's not surprising that this examination is not taking place. Since working out of flow takes so much time and energy, one really doesn't have time to sit back and reflect on what is really happening. The result is that despite the proficiency, the worker gets stressed and heads eventually, though directly, toward burnout. That's what happened to me at the museum. I was good at my job, but I was just nearly burnt out.

Being extremely efficient or competent at something doesn't mean you're in flow.

People become proficient in something they're not naturally good at because of ego or security needs. They also become proficient at entire jobs because they're naturally quite good at certain elements of them. This happens a lot in organizations with a prevailing culture of multi-tasking. Thus, when someone isn't good at something, her company sends her off to training courses to strengthen an area of "weakness" — something that doesn't come naturally to her and that she's often simply not interested in. Business owners can make this mistake because they assume nobody else knows the business as well as they do, or could do some of these other tasks as well as they can. There's also the financial reality, especially with start-ups, which are cash poor; many owners fail to realize that it may be cheaper in the long run to get someone else to do those jobs they're not so good at — someone who can do them in a fraction of the time, leaving owners free to generate more income by using their time to do the things they excel at.

In my case, I've had many jobs in which I was good at part, but not all, of the tasks; or enjoyed some, but not all, of them. At one point I was a wine industry information officer, so I was constantly responding to e-mails and phone calls, which certainly appealed to the Deal Maker in me. But the job offered no face-to-face contact with clients, so ultimately I was unfulfilled.

As a regional manager for a specialist medical college, my work was mainly on a computer in a one-person office; in many ways it was the most isolating job I'd ever had. It was also de-energizing. In my career at the art museum, I worked with ten curators who were cataloging forty thousand works of art for a database. It was my job to make sure the work was consistent and to refine the systems, which kept me out of flow. However, at this job we also put together exhibitions for international tours. It was my job to negotiate the venues, organize the tour and actually go on the tour with the works of art. That was great! There was a lot of variety, and many opportunities to connect with other people. Timing was everything, so this aspect was very much a Deal Maker's job, and I loved it. But still, I wasn't fully happy — or happy all of the time — because I didn't know precisely what it was that made me happy. Then I did my profile.

I was totally transformed when I learned I was a Deal Maker. It gave me permission to have fun, to put myself out into the world more and to be the person I was deep down inside, rather than someone who had taken on the characteristics of her role. It was such a revelation. Part of the revelation was in clarification of the past. Looking back, I could see that I was happiest when I had a lot of connection with people. And I was able to understand why all my previous work with numbers and figures de-energized me. While at the specialist medical college, I had to look after the accounts using QuickBooks, and that job so thoroughly drained me that I would put it off and put it off until the last possible moment, which only drained me more.

Shortly after learning my profile, I launched a global company in my own city totally based on my own existing networks, and relationships I'd developed over the years. That I was able to do so was such a revelation; it solidly confirmed what being in flow as a Dealmaker is all about. Involvement with that global company led me back into the training and coaching arena. In the past, I'd been trained in and worked with several energy healing modalities, and so in that respect was something of a healer. I'd scaled down on that type of healing work because of the nature of the healer/client relationship, and I had found the work somewhat isolating.

But I thought that if I could heal with words, the results might be markedly different. I had been a counselor in the therapy field for periods in my life; I'd also taught workshops on stress management and various healing modalities and done a lot of informal coaching. I've always known I was an effective counselor. During training, I was told I was so natural that it seemed I'd been doing it for years. So I decided I wanted to formalize my counseling, and use my experience to coach women in finding work they might like, or help them transition out of unrewarding jobs and into working in their passion and flow. Deal Makers create wonderful, safe environments for things to happen. When they come from heart-centeredness, Deal Makers make extraordinary transformational coaches and facilitators.

> *I was totally transformed when I learned I was a Deal Maker. It gave me permission to have fun, to put myself out into the world more and to be the person I was deep down inside, rather than someone who had taken on the characteristics of her role.*

When I'm teaching or coaching, it's paramount that I create a beautiful environment. A beautiful physical environment is created aurally with an absence of distracting sound, and visually by clean lines, the absence of clutter and often a window overlooking a peaceful garden or a natural landscape with trees. A harmonious space is vital for people to engage in transformational work and gain self-awareness. Energetically, a Deal Maker has a combination of sensory thinking, good timing, people-orientation and a desire for connection, all of which help to create the safe, harmonious space. Deal Makers are often known for their ability to hold space in a group situation. One-on-one, Deal Makers are gifted listeners, adding value by asking themselves how they can assist the other person to become more resourceful.

For instance, one of my clients, a Trader profile who was a government employee, told me in a session that she wanted to be an entrepreneur in property investments. I advised her that since this was a big-ticket item, that she may want to first trade smaller items to get into flow. So we talked about how to organize, and how to approach her research. After our session, she told me that she got a lot out of what we discussed, adding that the environment was crucial to the process.

During my coaching sessions, I ask people basic questions regarding their professions. When you are working, do you feel happy, effervescent? Do you look forward to certain aspects of your job over others? What duties leave you feeling drained? If someone is not happy, clearly the job's not working. But sometimes people don't have the freedom to just leave their jobs. So I help people understand their natural talents in a profile debriefing session, and develop a strategy to help them get into flow, examining the potential in work or business to redesign or outsource those tasks they don't. They are then able to pursue those aspects that come naturally and are most enjoyable. The ensuing teamwork has a great flow, and the synergy gained is awesome.

> *When they come from heart-centeredness, Deal Makers make extraordinary transformational coaches and facilitators.*

Another client was good at what she did, but it didn't make her happy. She was a psychologist who'd been in clinical practice for twenty years and felt bogged down. She wanted to design and teach workshops, but instead she worked one-on-one with clients. She couldn't get out of her situation because she was trapped by paperwork — sorting, collating, filing — even tax returns, some of which she'd not done for years. Any spare moment was devoted to her whirlwind of papers, or feeling completely immobilized by them. Her profile is Creator. Once she understood her strengths and the team she needed, she immediately hired a Mechanic to do all of that paperwork. She also got someone else to do all of her marketing, and soon after her business soared. Now she travels all over the country, creating and conducting incredible workshops — and she couldn't be happier. Similarly, I am now thrilled with my professional life. I have embraced my profile, and that has helped me understand why all those past careers didn't work for me. I am really in flow as a Deal Maker, and I love connecting people to other people and making win-win deals happen.

Some people mistakenly believe that Deal Makers spend most of their time on the phone, but it's not true. Deal Makers shine when building relationships face to face — which is why I am having lots of coffee dates these days! Nothing lights me up more than sharing what I've learned with women who get it; women who know that I once sat where they sit; women eager to make the transformational professional changes I was able to make.

So I ask you this again — does your job make you happy? If not, what job would?

Judy Hamilton is a coach and trainer, specializing in empowering women ready for transformational change. A facilitator of transformational events, Judy is dedicated to empowering women to get into flow and live the life they desire. She is also passionate about bringing positive progress in the areas of environmental sustainability, social justice and spiritual fulfillment. Judy has a business background in the visual arts, the wine industry, the healthcare industry and the non-profit sector. She holds a Bachelor of Arts in psychology and a postgraduate diploma in clinical hypnosis, and is a qualified master trainer and master coach in neuro-linguistic programming (NLP). Judy is also a certified Wealth Dynamics Master Practitioner, a Reiki master and a Pachamama Alliance facilitator. To learn more about Judy, visit www.JudyHamilton.com.au.

Real Estate Investing in Profile

STEVEN KHONG WITH JACKIE WONG

When people meet my wife, Jackie, and me, they encounter an unusual partnership. Two Lords, very happily married and running a business together? Yes! It's true. Our dual-Lord dynamic actually makes for a really fun and effectual partnership, in both business and marriage. And knowing ourselves as Lord profiles has dramatically and beneficially changed our approach to business. Partners in all things, Jackie and I have been real estate investors for several years. Before we knew about Wealth Dynamics, before we knew we were Lords, we invested in properties before they were built, buying them from developers in desirable areas.

Though we didn't know it when we began buying properties, our knowledge of real estate investment was coming from an Accumulator perspective. We were using Accumulator strategy. This is a common approach in Malaysia; accumulate property in order to sell at a profit. The news surrounding us was filled with stories of big payoffs. Development was happening at terrific speeds. Jackie and I were both ready to quit our jobs in advertising and IT management (respectively) and move on to something more fun, exciting and challenging. The timing was right, the climate seemed great — so we went ahead without considering whether we were in flow or not.

We bought a property with no money down and waited three years for it to be built. When we purchased the property, the area surrounding it was undeveloped. But during our wait, other developments sprang up around our own, changing the perceived value of our property. We found ourselves stuck with a white elephant, locked into a project we couldn't do anything about for at least three years. All we could do was look on in horror, anticipating what might happen once the property was delivered. And of course there was no cash flow coming in from the investment because the property wasn't ready to be rented or sold. Our money was tied up with the developer, and with multiple mortgages to pay each month, we remained salaried employees at jobs we'd outgrown.

In the midst of this learning experience, Jackie and I discovered Wealth Dynamics. When we found out we are both Lords, Jackie remembered that, as a kid, she loved helping out at school fundraisers and events — she realized that she'd always been happiest when she was collecting money. And I recalled that I'd been class treasurer, as well as treasurer for most organizations I'd been involved in! People trust me with their money, and I've always preferred to stay out of the spotlight and manage the details. Real estate investment seemed like a natural fit for both of us. So why did it also seem so stressful?

The timing was right, the climate seemed great — so we went ahead without considering whether we were in flow or not.

One day I read a story about a gardener who made a living collecting rent from everyone in his village. Something about the story struck me — and then Jackie and I met Roger Hamilton. We told him about our experiences investing. He agreed that real estate was a great business for us, but that our strategy was failing because we were not investing *according* to our profiles. We were using Accumulator strategy, not Lord strategy. We had yet to really enter our flow.

Of course! Lords, above all, crave certainty. They want to know exactly what their cash flow will be every month, not wait for years to make a profit they can't even be sure will materialize; the risk is too stressful. Roger drew up a simple plan: if we bought a property for a hundred-thousand dollars and it brought in a positive cash flow of a thousand dollars in rent each month, what would happen if we had four, five, six of these properties?

There is a right investment strategy for every profile. For Lords, it is to grow our wealth through increasing cash flows. So we changed our strategy. We began buying completed properties to tenant immediately, collecting rental fees right away. When we bought our first rental property, we felt awesome — like winners. At thirty percent below market value, the apartment was a great deal, especially since we were able to rent it at forty percent above our mortgage payment after fixing it up. Our tenant is still there after four years. He's great about paying his rent on time, so we're prompt in seeing to repairs. It's a symbiotic relationship — and we love the steady income! Within our first three years of investing according to profile, we were able to purchase enough of these positive-cash-flow properties to leave our jobs. The stress melted away. Now, being paid every month, we have a month-long window in which to make course corrections with any of our properties, as opposed to the old method of waiting years to make changes and worrying over uncertainties the whole time. This change has brought us great joy and made our work even more fun than we imagined it could be.

Following our hearts and having fun also means spending time serving the people around us. Now, after years of proven success investing according to profile, Jackie and I are real estate investment coaches in addition to managing our own properties. We help others invest according to profile, so they get the most satisfaction and profit from their investments. When you discover your investment flow through profile, time and energy are instantly freed up. Instead of running after money, you get to enjoy spending energy in giving back to the world.

There is a right investment strategy for every profile. For Lords, it is to grow our wealth through increasing cash flows. So we changed our strategy.

All our new clients take the Wealth Dynamics profile test. From that point, we can gauge a person's strengths and interests, mapping out an ideal investment plan for the client based on her profile. The foundation of our recommendations, of course, will always be that there is a positive cash flow coming in, especially in trying economic times. That makes sense, for every profile! It's great fun to work with investors from their profiles. A Creator profile, for example, loves to play with properties over which he can have creative influence. He probably wants to invest in a variety of buildings, especially those that are a little run-down, so he can knock out some walls, add stories and put in new floors and different lighting. He'll also love to brainstorm ideas for improving cash flow.

Our client, Nick, is a Creator. Nick's greatest value is not in doing the nitty gritty, detailed work of sourcing, researching, evaluating or managing proper-ties; it is in the richness of his creative input. He's quick to generate ideas and solutions, and intently focused on the big picture and end goal. Nick entrusts us with his property investment portfolio and looks forward to the security of a safe investment that he and his family can access in twenty years' time. We not only located Nick's property and made sure it fit his profile and his goals, we help him to fully manage that property by making sure it is always tenanted, rentals are paid on time and the property is maintained in great condition. Nick has creative control and peace of mind about meeting his future goals, so he's happy about his investment.

When you discover your investment flow through profile, time and energy are instantly freed up. Instead of running after money, you get to enjoy spending energy in giving back to the world.

Other clients of ours, a wealthy Star/Creator couple, were already into prop-erty investment before they met us. They thought it was a good idea, but they didn't know why; they bought interesting and glamorous properties through sheer instinct, not knowing what to do or how to deal with them. Some were vacant, some were in other towns and therefore difficult to rent and look after. And their money was all tied up in this confusing, scattered web of properties that lacked cash flow. Through awareness of their profiles, we helped them determine their life objectives, and then how their property investments could and should serve and support those objectives.

They didn't have children yet but wanted to. So together we came up with the objective of planning their long-term wealth portfolio. Over time, Jackie and I have helped them hone their portfolio. We've urged them to sell far-flung and under-performing properties and develop, instead, a dynamic set of properties in good locations that will see excellent capital appreciation in the years to come. Now they feel a sense of ease, knowing their children will be well provided for.

The future is unknown, but we can know who we are. Finding your natural flow is the wisdom that will guide you to wealth, and anything is possible — and great fun — when you let your profile direct your strategy!

Steven Khong has been happily married to Jackie Wong since 2000. They are property investment coaches and consultants based in Malaysia, serving clients around the world through their company, Simfoni Dinamik. Building on their in-depth knowledge of the property investment arena and Wealth Dynamics profiling, Steven and Jackie have a hands-on approach that enables clients to build and preserve wealth in a fun, stress-free way.

Steven is a certified XL Life and Wealth Coach and was nominated for the XL Results Foundation's Extraordinary Lives Award in 2007. In 2008, he won the award for Malaysia in recognition of his support of a school for the visually impaired. He wrote his first computer program at the age of twelve, and worked in the IT field for seventeen years, rising from the programming ranks to become a manager. He loves traveling around the world with Jackie, connecting and inspiring entrepreneurs, and supporting educational and social causes. To learn more about Steven and Jackie, and their company, please visit www.SDPropertyInvest.com.

The Soul Safari

DR. NANCY BRANDT

My purpose in life has been clear to me since I was tiny: I have always wanted to shine a light through the darkness, helping animals and their guardians to heal and fully experience their commitment to each other. Even as a child, I sensed how much animals have to teach their human partners. Animals are pure soul energy. They have no need for judgment or expectation. They don't label themselves or others. They are always in pure flow, acting from the centers of themselves. Animals offer us a priceless gift: unconditional relationship, a place where we can find our own essence, our own soul's purpose, our ability to relate.

As a holistic veterinarian I've had the joy of working with animals and their people all over the world. One of my most memorable experiences was working with extraordinary elephants in Thailand. They'd had parts of their feet blown off by landmines, and had been fitted with prostheses. Their wounds, however, weren't healing; they remained infected, and the prostheses were unusable. The devoted handlers were devastated — their elephant friends might have to be destroyed if they didn't get help soon. Our team went to work, creating special blends of essential oils to heal the tissue faster. Before long, the animals had healed and were able to walk with the help of their prostheses.

This is just one beautiful example of the myriad of successful experiences I've had in blending traditional allopathic medicine with other healing methods. It's all thanks to having and utilizing a full toolbox, which always includes a network of experienced practitioners helping one another advance their base of knowledge. As a Master Practitioner of Wealth Dynamics, I see that the same holds true in any context. The relationship of collaboration and teamwork produces sustainable and rewarding results. When we use our profiles as scaffolding for building our dreams, we are always in flow.

As a Creator, I'm naturally curious about everything. And for me, as for any Creator, relationship is the most dynamic, creative learning experience there is. The more fascinated with animal behavior I've become, the more interested in human behavior I am, too. There is no separation between the human and animal worlds; just a perceived separation, which I choose to bridge in my work with everyone I encounter. My commitment to the human-animal bond has led me to Master Practitioner training in Wealth Dynamics. Arriving in Bali, looking out the window of the cab, I saw evidence of monkeys and elephants everywhere. I was like a kid in a candy store! I couldn't wait for my day off, so I could go and play with them. Witnessing animals in their wonderfully specific energies can teach us about our own patterns of behavior. And these lessons connect perfectly with our profiles!

When we use our profiles as scaffolding for building our dreams, we are always in flow.

In the seminar, I thought to myself, "What could I offer to Bali and its beauty?" Wealth Dynamics had been a springboard for me to rediscover my true purpose. I was excitedly awaiting my trip to experience the Bali animals. I was eager to see what they would teach me, and to give them love. I invited my fellow seminar attendees to come with me. Ten of them came, thinking I was giving a seminar of my own. Thank God I'm a Creator and could make it up on the fly! We headed to the monkey sanctuary.

Monkey energy is spring energy, very fast-paced and energetic. It brings you up. Anything is possible! "What are we going to do next?" is the great monkey question. The monkeys jumped all over us, eating with no fear or hesitation the bananas we'd bought. Baby monkeys climbed a tree and jumped into the water below, splashing each other and having a ball. Being with the monkeys was a profound experience for everyone. I shared a couple of techniques for soaking up that spring-monkey energy, and the rest was just experiential. Our debriefing session was beautiful, and taught all of us. Then we were off to be with the elephants.

Elephant energy is pure commitment, pure wisdom and a deep ground-edness. An elephant will have one handler for life. And she will never forget that person, even if he leaves. The bond between handlers and their elephant friends is like that between parents and children — the Thai handlers we'd helped hadn't been able to bear the idea of putting their charges down. The bond was that solid.

You can imagine the energy difference between monkeys and elephants! The difference is much like that between a Creator and an Accumulator. We all sat down and debriefed after we'd visited the gentle giants. I asked my Wealth Dynamics colleagues, "How did that feel? What did it do to feed your soul?" They encouraged me: "You should do this all the time!" Driving back, a group of Master Practitioners collectively came up with a name for what we'd experi-enced: a "Soul Safari." We had discovered a new kind of safari: a journey toward using our unconditional relationships with animals as a means to discovering who we are, and finding the truth of our own souls.

Witnessing animals in their wonderfully specific energies can teach us about our own patterns of behavior. And these lessons connect perfectly with our profiles!

With animals, everything is based on intuition. In my work I'm continually observing my clients and their animals, seeing what's happening in their bodies based on their belief systems and where they are directing their energy. Wealth Dynamics has streamlined this process in a remarkable way. Guardian profiles are my launching point for understanding each guardian's particular flow of energy, and how interruptions in that flow may be affecting the animal's health.

Take, for example, one of my client-guardians, Meg. A classic Lord, she's introverted, in need of certainty, explanation and clear process at all times. Lords need their animals to feed them with the certainty they crave. In Meg's case, her pet's efforts to meet this need were making the animal sick. Meg was in retail, a profession that required her to be extroverted and create many relationships. This was totally off-profile, and it was stressing her terribly. She'd come home and dump that energy on her pet. Through experience, I was convinced that this was blocking her animal's ability to heal. I was able, through offering data and assurance (so important for a Lord), to show Meg that she needed to make changes in her own energy. When she analyzed what I presented, she realized it was true. She actually went back to school and changed her profession, becoming a medical transcriptionist. Now, Meg works from home, is making good money (always important for a Lord) and is not over-taxed by an excess of social contact. She loves what she does, and her animal benefits too.

We had discovered a new kind of safari: a journey toward using our unconditional relationships with animals as a means to discovering who we are, and finding the truth of our own souls.

The principles of Wealth Dynamics make it easier to communicate. If you are talking with a Lord, like Meg, and you're unconcerned with methodology, they'll think you're insane. But if you say, "I am certain that we can take step one, step two and step three, and get these results," the guardian with a Lord profile will be so relieved! Speaking to each client through her profile and natural flow language puts her at ease, helps work through panic about health issues and opens her mind to new opportunities and modalities for healing.

If I can approach guardians each in their own flow-language, they can hear and accept that their own energy may be a factor in their animal's health, vibrancy and happiness. And, ultimately, they will connect it to their own patterns of belief and behavior! I will do profiles for clients only when I am working with them in a coaching context. Many of my guardian clients choose coaching along with veterinary consultation. With a grasp of the power of energy, and the power of the bond between themselves and their animal companions, sometimes they'll recognize that they don't even need to bring the animals in! Instead, they'll tell me, "Let's talk and work on my energy blocks" — the very issues that are impacting their animals' well-being. The bond between animals and humans is inextricable from animals' health. After all, the animal does not bring itself to the vet!

Before Wealth Dynamics, I did everything myself. I would focus on too many things and dilute my effectiveness. My energy was all over the place, chasing after every shiny new idea and neglecting what I had already built before it had time to take root. When I learned that the cycles of industry are a natural flow from spring to summer to fall to winter to spring again, I found a natural path to take my ideas from larval stage to butterfly. Awareness of this cycle became my guide, my map.

Today, assured of the power of my intuition as a Creator, I have built a team based on where my various businesses lie within that cycle. For example, at the moment my clinic itself is in winter. Knowing this is part of a cycle, and that spring will come again, I hired a Lord to keep the cash flowing while I focus on my passion and my purpose: helping my clients and their animals heal and experience vibrancy.

What we're really healing here is our souls, our centers. By shifting our belief systems through embracing who we really are, we find a true path to health for our companion animals and ourselves. It is the animals themselves who lead us to our path. On the Soul Safari that is our birthright, they lovingly guide us, as our compassionate relatives.

Dr. Nancy Brandt, DVM, CVA, CAC, is a holistic veterinarian, medical intuitive and Certified Animal Chiropractor and Acupuncturist who has dedicated her life to helping animals and their guardians lead fulfilling lives and enjoy each moment they have together. She is an entrepreneur, life navigator and philanthropist who travels the world to further her education and give back to the animal community. Nancy is a Master Practitioner of NLP (neuro-linguistic programming) and Wealth Dynamics, and offers coaching to clients and healers in possibility thinking, self-healing, abundance and natural flow. She now offers Soul Safari journeys for those who wish to find purpose. To learn more about Nancy, please visit www.NancyBrandtDVM.com and www.TheCenterOfSelf.com.

Home Is
Where Your Wealth Is

GINA LAZENBY

Twenty-first century businesswomen face an extraordinary opportunity. Because the traditional, winner-takes-all paradigm does not allow for sustainability, the world's financial systems are experiencing dramatic change, even crumbling. It's clear that a different approach is necessary; and it's a great time to enlist the genius of women in creating it.

Women's psyches are geared to the collective: the family, the community, the greater good. The inherent ability of women to cooperate and collaborate is essential to the health of any home or social community. And if women nurture, value and develop those skills in themselves, they'll have them to role model for others, which is especially useful in business now. We can blaze the trail for a new way of doing business that nourishes *everyone*.

If we want to survive and even thrive in business — and in society at large — it's time to bring that feminine wisdom, and the language of collaboration, to the world of commerce. After decades of operating in a business world largely built on greed and fear of lack, however, many women have lost their fluency in the language of cooperation and their trust in their own wisdom. It's time for women to gather together, step forward and support each other in reconnecting with themselves, their natural flow and the reasons why they began their great journeys in the first place. It's time for them to start from the ground up, building sustainable, balanced and joyful lives. It's time for us to come home to our foundations and look at everything differently.

Home has so many facets of meaning. There's the home we humans find within our relationship to the rest of nature and its cycles; our physical homes, which reflect who we are; and the home we find within ourselves when we are in flow, valuing ourselves for who we are and pursuing that which makes our hearts sing. This last, the spiritual home we'll never lose nor leave, is the one to build and strengthen first.

In my work with women in business, I've seen that women are wonderfully nurturing and supportive of others. They can also be great at self-deprecation and sacrifice, and they are more comfortable identifying their own weaknesses than they are at taking credit for their achievements. Ask a woman, "Who are you? What do you do?" and she may not see or articulate her own value, even if others regard her as a world leader in her niche. This occurs on a universal level among the women who attend my workshops.

Seeing this amongst even the most talented and accomplished women we know, my colleagues and I have created what we call a Business Fingerprint. The Fingerprint is a web resource that coaches people to express, very briefly and clearly, who they are, what they're great at and what their needs are right now (another especially difficult one for women). If you really understand what you're the go-to person for, others will come and find you and invite you to do what you're great at.

If we want to survive and even thrive in business — and in society at large — it's time to bring that feminine wisdom, and the language of collaboration, to the world of commerce.

Wealth Dynamics profiles are inextricably linked with individual Fingerprints. Knowing your profile, you can say with confidence, "I'm a Star, which means I'm naturally good at being a public voice, particularly for what I'm passionate about." You can become more conscious of your competence. Say you're also passionate about health and interested in helping children. A Mechanic or Lord profile will meet you and say, "Wow! I do this work with children's health. I need a Star communicator. Perfect!" One short conversation will make it clear you can start to help each other.

This is especially important for women, who tend to try to do it all. My friend M.B., for example, is a Creator. M.B. worked tirelessly in someone else's business because she saw the technology's huge potential for future profitability, but because she was out of flow, she found no joy in it. When Wealth Dynamics helped her reconnect to what inspired her, she started a new enterprise, an accelerator for other ventures. She's allowed herself to be a true Creator, so her work now makes her heart sing. Wealth Dynamics gives people a language to use in accepting, celebrating and expressing who they are.

Wealth Dynamics gives people a language to use in accepting, celebrating and expressing who they are.

Home as tangible, as a physical place, may be more a part of women's consciousness than men's, but for everyone, home is a reflection of oneself. When I regard my own life, I see that everything I've done in the past several years around my home has extended out into the world, and vice versa. Years of study spent writing about and coaching Feng Shui has taught me that home life is the foundation for the rest of our lives. If the home life doesn't work, nothing else works either.

It's not sustainable for women, who are often professionals and primary caregivers, to sacrifice quality of home and family life for success in business. Success without stress should be the function of our homes and our businesses. Otherwise we're giving up what feeds and nurtures us. We'll try to function as usual, caring for everyone else first, and exhaust ourselves in the process. But there's no real dynamism to offer the world when we're attempting to draw water from an empty well.

What we can glean from the ancient wisdom in Feng Shui and Wealth Dynamics, both of which are rooted in the I Ching, is a deep knowledge of cycles and seasons, and the energy of each as they relate to our pursuits. Finding a flow with the seasons is accessing that last and essential form of home, the home we find in ourselves as deeply connected to the natural world. To grow businesses and find joy in our lives, we need sustainability. Thinking about sustainability requires looking at nature, embracing its power and influence. How does nature make things work? If we just look out the window, all the answers are there.

We don't have to invent anything. We just need to remember.

Should I put my plant in the greenhouse, feed it chemical fertilizers and light it twenty-four hours a day so it grows at lightning speed? Or should I find an environment that suits it, and watch it grow? Which plant will deliver the fruit that nourishes me on the deepest levels? It's the one grown in the natural cycle, not the one that's being forced. We can force anything — and have, for decades — but we see now that we can, using the wisdom of the feminine, reinvent our world, rather than wait for some inevitable collapse.

Coming home to ourselves brings a solid foundation to whatever we do, creating an essential flow between the health and harmony of our homes and our businesses that ripples ever outward in the world. The challenge to women, and everyone, is to rise to that opportunity and support each other in reinventing our world — from the inside out.

A former PR and marketing consultant with thirty-plus years experience in the business world, Gina Lazenby is a Wealth Dynamics Master Practitioner for Women in Business and the author of the bestselling The Feng Shui House Book, Simple Feng Shui and The Healthy Home, which have sold over half a million copies worldwide. She launched the Feng Shui Society and the Feng Shui Network and developed the world's first professional training program for this ancient wisdom. Gina has spoken and taught on Feng Shui, Personal Change and Life & Business Flow on five continents. She offers educational retreats for women at her specially designed "Healthy Home" in Yorkshire, England, based on the themes of wellness, wisdom and wealth.

Gina's new business, Gaia Gold, is developing a new technology platform to support more effective online collaboration using the Business Fingerprint. To learn more about Gina's work, visit her blog at GinaLazenby.wordpress.com and website www. GinaLazenby.com.

Focusing on Flow

SUE BARLEY, PH.D.

My passion is human transformation — helping people, particularly at this time of human evolution, to be able to transform elegantly into the people they were always meant to be. Can you imagine bringing the world your gifts and achieving success by being who you really are, rather than the person you think you should or ought to be? What sort of world would we be living in if most people were truly able to operate from their resonant, creative selves? What decisions would be made? Who would we connect with? What would we be doing with our time? We can imagine the great changes that might occur in the world if we were all operating from our true selves.

So when I came across Wealth Dynamics, I was totally blown away by what it has to offer us. Here is an ancient system linked by genius creator Roger Hamilton to the flow of wealth and resources. How extraordinary. And the focus is on our natural, gifted-by-the-universe talents. These are the talents that we are often not even aware of — or worse, ignore as we focus on fixing our weaknesses.

At school we were encouraged to become good at everything and spend time improving weaker areas like math, sports or science. We thought we needed to correct and mend ourselves, rather than realizing we were actually already rather wonderful. We just weren't looking in the right direction.

Those of us in the training and coaching professions have spent many years working to improve ourselves — the emphasis always being on self-improvement, not self-acceptance. Yet how much easier could life be if we were to follow the flow of who we really are? We are all born with skills, attributes and talents that make us each individually special, with individual gifts to bring to the world. And at this time, the world needs our whole selves more than ever, blind spots and all.

After years spent exploring different transformational therapies, I found Wealth Dynamics to be a door-opener. It gave me permission to follow my flow and to stop berating myself and spending energy on things I wasn't! I wasn't a natural accountant; I wasn't a natural negotiator; I wasn't a natural systems thinker. These are all gifts that belong to other people. I was, however, a natural "enthuser" and motivator. But by spending all my energies on things I *wasn't*, I had become less able to access and use the gifts I did have!

Those of us in the training and coaching professions have spent many years working to improve ourselves — the emphasis always being on self-improvement, not self-acceptance.

In the recent past, a lot of my work was in helping individuals transform. Sometimes just helping someone rediscover her natural interests, talents and gifts was enough to help her move forward. Others needed a little more help finding the essence of who they really are — the people they were before they took on other people's expectations and views. Many years working with individuals using the latest transformational tools showed me that Wealth Dynamics is a fabulous compass to help them re-orient back to their fundamental selves.

Most of us have taken on ideas, traits and burdens from outside ourselves that hamper our own flow. But why should our problems be our focal point? How does that really serve our growth? In our natural flow, our natural selves, we experience ease. The right resources and people are attracted to us and respond to us. For me, Wealth Dynamics was a gift: it gave me an indicator of where my flow could be found and, importantly, what strategy I could adopt to make best use of it.

We all know that we most attract what we focus on. So if we focus entirely on removing problems, or "blocks," we lose the opportunity to find the easy pathway or route ahead. The trick is to find the ways to flow around the blocks and rocks with ease and effortlessness. In my work with others, I once spent most of the time focused on removing blocks. Now I've realized that finding the flow around the block can be just as transformational! And oftentimes rather easier, too. A big part of flowing around a block, rather than letting it get in your way, is to recognize that one person's block is another's opportunity. In other words, it's time to focus on who we are and what we have, rather than who we are not and what we don't have.

My professional life has really transformed through embracing Wealth Dynamics. At a certain point, I realized I was playing way too small — and I still found everything difficult. I was creating minimal attraction to myself and my services, knowing all the while I had something of tremendous value to offer. I was out there chasing the butterflies! Despite trying everything that the marketing "experts" recommended, my business was not thriving. And it all seemed like very hard work indeed.

Finally, a shift resulting from my work with Wealth Dynamics changed everything. I discovered that I enjoyed speaking and communicating about all dimensions of human growth and transformation. And once I allowed myself full rein to do this work, opportunities for speaking and writing started to appear.

Most of us have taken on ideas, traits and burdens from outside ourselves that hamper our own flow. But why should our problems be our focal point? How does that really serve our growth?

My profile gave me confidence in the natural abilities I already knew I wanted to stretch and cultivate. All of us sometimes need an external push to help guide us to an internal reality. And Wealth Dynamics did that for me. Knowing myself as a Star, I can now grant myself automatic permission to go out there and shine a light on all the things I find interesting and important. By doing so, I am helping other people too — how cool is that? Now, in flow, I spend my time being enthusiastic and communicating from the heart in ways that support and enhance the growth of others. If you are finding some aspects of your life a struggle, some key questions to ask yourself are: Are you playing big enough? Are you focusing on your natural flow — or are you focusing on what's wrong with you?

I am often asked by people who run their own businesses, "If I focus on my flow, what about all the other jobs that need to be done?" This is a great question. Any job you find a block or challenge is likely to be in someone else's flow! By focusing on your own flow, you will fully discover where you need to bring other people in to help you, creating opportunities for yourself and others all at the same time! It really couldn't be more perfect.

In other words, it's time to focus on who we are and what we have, rather than who we are not and what we don't have.

We are at a unique place in time and history wherein old systems and structures are changing to make way for a new era. This is a time, more than ever, when being clear about your role and purpose for being on this planet is critical. Who you are as a fully engaged and purposeful being may be just what we all need right now.

My advice: demonstrate YOUR gifts, follow your flow and be a benefit to all of us! So what's your flow? What's your passion?

Dr. Sue Barley is one of the new energy teachers bringing forward intuitive insights and learnings to help re-empower humanity. Sue began her career of discovery as a research scientist with a PhD in chemistry. She has since trained in and practiced a variety of transformational change approaches, spanning the realms of science, health, wealth and spirituality. As a speaker and a Star, Sue has trained and coached internationally for several global corporations and delighted audiences worldwide. An enthusiastic communicator, Sue has a passion to help people re-discover their true inner brilliance and their reconnection with their soul. She provides private guidance sessions and, as an author and speaker, shares her insights with others. Visit www.SueBarley.com to learn more.

Swimming Lessons for Flow

ADRIAN PONNAMPALAM

Many people feel stuck in life, bogged down like they can't move. This is often because they invested so much to climb whatever ladder they're on that they feel it costs too much to let go. Sometimes they are too weighed down by obligations, financial and otherwise, and sometimes they feel they have no support. I know what this is like; I've been there.

People who are bogged down don't pursue changes that they could and should make because they are overwhelmed by the big picture. Instead of looking at the next step in the process of changing their lives, they look to the end goal, and it seems so far away that the distance paralyzes them. This often happens when people first encounter Wealth Dynamics. Many do their profile but do not then absorb and apply the new information, because they are preoccupied with how far ahead their perceived mentors, like Donald Trump or Oprah, seem to be.

The problem is that they think the only way to success is to jump into the raging river. That's fine if you're equipped and trained for the task, but it's not the only way. The approach that worked for me was building a solid foundation in much the same way I learned to swim — effectively moving, one stroke at a time, from the calm waters into the river — and on to the beach of dreams and goals.

When I got out of college and got a job, I immediately bought a house. My parents helped me do that, but the ultimate responsibility was still mine. And so began my life of obligation, not only to the upkeep and care of my only and largest investment, but also to pay back the loan from my parents. During this time, I also suffered a high level of stress at work, largely because the job wasn't what I thought it'd be. But my financial obligations were such that I didn't really see how I could pursue anything different. I was stuck. About this time, I also suffered from a huge personal crisis. I was truly at my wits' end.

I thought my world had collapsed from under me, but I learned that it's often when we are most vulnerable or have a lot at stake that we are most teachable, or coachable. My frustration led me to register for a personal development workshop, which was my first experience of the right type of education and coaching for me. I realized I wasn't living my life; rather, I was surviving the expectations of my environment and other peoples' values. So I wiped my slate clean and started to participate on the playing field of life. I sought mentors who would teach. I devoured information in the areas of equities trading, property investment and business, resulting in the expansion of my financial portfolio and expertise. I was enabled to try more things in a short space of time than I had in all my previous years pursuing a professional career.

I thought my world had collapsed from under me, but I learned that it's often when we are most vulnerable or have a lot at stake that we are most teachable, or coachable.

Discovering my Wealth Dynamics profile was significant, a story of self-discovery in itself. When I looked at my profile graph, I noticed that my strength was mainly in the Deal Maker area. The next strongest indication was in the Supporter area. Most profiles are strong in one area and a little bit less on the left and right, but my results actually skewed one way — to the right side of the square. My Wealth Dynamics profile helped me discover my true inherent value. The chains of preconceived notions I had about career, wealth and life started to fall away. I was learning to swim, to get into my flow.

Knowing that I was a Deal Maker with a strong Supporter streak allowed me to realize that I am people-oriented, which guided me to be what I'd always wanted: a coach. And I realized that, through my volunteer work, I'd already been coaching people for a while. Thank goodness I'd invested time and effort in discovering my true **value**. We are all born with a gold mine of talent that is often conditioned out of us when we were told to sit down, be quiet and follow orders! Discovering how to apply my true **value** is what made the difference.

My profile helped me fine-tune my strategy for wealth creation. In Roger's formula of **Wealth = Value x Leverage**, notice how **Value** comes first. Most people try to apply leverage to what they think is profitable without first discovering their own true **value**. That was my mistake. If you are not clear on the **value** you bring to a strategy, it often turns out to be a poor strategy. It was clear to me that I had to stop spending time and energy working hard at equities trading and other activities that were out of my flow. I started to ask the right questions: "Why am I here?" "What is it that I want to create in life?" "Who do I want to BE?" "Who can I help?" "Where can I contribute?" These were life-changing questions for me.

When coaching, I'm in the flow and often coach people at a highly intuitive level. This used to surprise me, but now I know that coaching is my **value**. The result is that the client is moved and becomes inspired to act. When I'm in that moment, the flow experience, I feel that it's the Supporter me. I express my Deal Maker side through collaborative marketing and also through the way I put ideas together for my clients. All my newfound education culminated when I created NextStep Coaching to help people start to change. As a wealth catalyst coach, I assist people who feel stuck and overwhelmed to make a major change. I don't throw my clients into the raging river; instead, I use NextStep Coaching, taking them to the next level by teaching them to swim first. It's practical and achievable.

> *Some people* leverage *far too early. If there's not enough* value, *then leveraging could be dangerous. It could also be fruitless if others don't see what your* value *is because it wasn't strongly established.*

One client was a counselor who wanted to double her income. She did individual consultations and lectured in a niche of psychotherapy, but she hated lecturing because she found it draining. She wanted to quit that job and just get more clients. We discovered that her Wealth Dynamics profile was a Star with a strong creative streak; that means her **value** is in her quick-thinking, outward-focused personality.

The problem was that her class lectures were just too structured, which is how she had been trained. Taking action with her profile, we shifted her approach and facilitated the educational process using the power of her personality. Now when she walks into class, she asks questions, moderates student responses and inspires students to be their best, simply by being herself. Her passion for the subject was always there — I got her back to her heart, where her **value** lies, so that now she loves her classes.

We stabilized her business, too. She had an average business with an ad hoc number of clients who simply paid per session, so her revenue was unpredictable. We explored her business model and arranged counseling packages (which she'd never done before). We added value through collaborative marketing. The new model gave her a more structured business. Some people *leverage* far too early. If there's not enough *value*, then leveraging could be dangerous. It could also be fruitless if others don't see what your *value* is because it wasn't strongly established.

One client, a naturopath and international lecturer, did not realize her **value**. She just wanted more sales, as most businesses in the alternative health industry do not earn much. Her Wealth Dynamics profile revealed that she was a Trader. Her passion was to help people heal themselves, and she'd found a number of innovative products to assist them in that process. The next step was for her to have a Supporter take care of attracting and managing clients, to free her up to work on the business. She also began to outsource time-consuming and low-value activities. She'd loved putting together the healing programs, though, and had added so much **value** to them that it was attractive to clients and she was excited to offer them! Now that **value** was established, it was time to leverage through marketing.

Something interesting happened through that process. We encountered a recurring problem that had held this passionate and long-serving naturopath back: she had a self-image that prevented her from receiving the money she was worth. At first, she could not handle raising her prices. That's where I was able to add my own **value** as a coach, and assist her in turning that around. Then, as she started to work on her business rather than in her business, she was surprised to discover her interest in share market trading, with a strong potential for leverage. This is very much in alignment with her Trader profile. As she makes this transition, knowing her **value**, she can now start to learn and practice before jumping into the river.

One thing to expect is that whenever you set a goal for growth in any endeavor, you will discover new situations or problems. The purpose of this is for you to grow and define your place in the world. Another client was a high level executive for a consultancy. He was a full-time, highly paid employee, but felt very stuck. He had no freedom at work, and because of office politics, his relationships with his colleagues were strained. He wanted to replace his lucrative job with an Internet strategy, and had taken many courses costing a lot of money. The strange thing was, Internet marketing wasn't even his passion. But he thought it was a way out of his job and into a lifestyle of freedom, a change he was desperate to make.

> *One thing to expect is that whenever you set a goal for growth in any endeavor, you will discover new situations or problems. The purpose of this is for you to grow and define your place in the world.*

When we did his Wealth Dynamics profile, he was a Mechanic. This was no surprise to me, as it meshed with his skills and the way he talked. But what makes Wealth Dynamics work so well is that behind each person's profile is his why, his purpose in life. This client discovered his purpose is to grow collaborative communities with a strong environmental focus. When he found his **value**, he found his flow. What he got to see from the Wealth Dynamics profile was whom he needed in order to create a team that could achieve his purpose.

The thing is, he's brilliant at what he does, and he realized that the only way to earn the income he wanted was to keep his job. He didn't know his Mechanic skills were transferable. Once he learned his true **value**, he was able to leverage it. He remained at his job, but continues to plan and work for an inspiring future.

And because he knows who he is, he's able to apply his strength to any situation in and out of work. With his experience of taking action aligned with his flow, he now runs workshops, teaching environmentally sustainable strategies for city folk. He is creating his dream in a small way by staying connected with his why. He is happy — and that is true wealth. By the way, his work relationships improved as he changed.

Part of profiting from your full potential is to know WHO you are and WHY you are. When this is aligned, WHAT you are is powerful! Achievement is just a natural consequence when a fulfilling life is already being lived. Who you are is a combination of your profile and your purpose. I inspire people to live the life they love with freedom and make a difference in the world. It is my why. I know I get in the flow whenever I coach. I'm living my wealth.

And yet, all of those significant changes in my life came one step at a time. In today's economic climate, the reality is that many of us feel we simply cannot go anywhere else for work or do something fulfilling. By using Wealth Dynamics, we can discover a great deal about our true wealth, our authentic self. The Wealth Dynamics Enterprise Stages and Vector Cards add further insight into where you are, what is coming and how to prepare for it. With that knowledge, each of us can work toward a life of happiness and freedom *where we already are*, no matter where that is. That is the experience of flow.

Adrian Ponnampalam is a success coach for business owners, entrepreneurs and investors, much like an athletic coach. He believes that achievement is a natural consequence of a fulfilling life. The foundation of his empowering process is helping clients ensure that what they do is in alignment with who they are. Adrian assists clients through their Wealth Dynamics profile test and helps them figure out their NextStep. Adrian also puts a Deal Maker's spin on the value proposition and market connections of businesses. As an added value to his coaching service, Adrian can help businesses be sale and investor ready. To learn more about how Adrian's services can benefit you, visit www.Wealth CatalystCoach.com.

Finding Your Way

ANDY GREENHILL

I seek to empower people with the concept of becoming a twenty-first-century samurai. Too often, people think "samurai" and have visions of warriors who battled with swords, but the true meaning of samurai is "one who serves." The overriding purpose of a samurai was to serve his lord, and if that required the ultimate sacrifice of giving his life, then he was honored to serve by doing so.

When you discover what you are prepared to die for, you're ready to honor what you're destined to live for. Every day, we are living, but we are also dying. What we use each living moment of our day for is effectively what we are dying for. If we sit and watch TV all day, then we are giving our life for what we've watched. Every minute we spend is gone forever; however, every minute invested gives back with interest. The challenge lies in discovering what it is we are willing to give our lives for, our true purpose.

My purpose in this life is to share ancient wisdom for modern application. It is my passion. Specifically, I love helping people uncover and harness their full potential by elevating their own consciousness; I enjoy showing business leaders how to bring immediate and powerful changes to their companies; and I revel in teaching groups and individuals how to build an "Enduring Enterprise."

What do I mean by enduring? In martial arts we follow the code of Budo, the way of the warrior, an ancient system that has been passed from Master to Master for hundreds of years. Its core principles are so enduring that they translate successfully through many generations, transcending geographic and cultural borders. But within the parameters of these core principles, each student must find his own way to apply them.

The Japanese word Do is translated as "Way" (also referred to as Tao). Some years ago, I went to Canada for some intense training in Budo. On my arrival, my Master, the remarkable Yamanaka Shihan, asked, "What are your questions, Andy?" I said, "Sensei, I just want to learn more about the Way." He shook his head. "Andy, Andy, Andy. There is no Way. There is only your Way." Those nine words caused a massive paradigm shift for me.

On my path, I have encountered an alarming number of people trying to live the life others expect them to live. Each of us has our own path that we are destined to follow. The path one follows through martial arts is one dimension, but the principles can be applied universally in all aspects of life, including business.

The challenge lies in discovering what it is we are willing to give our lives for, our true purpose.

Wealth Dynamics allows you to understand more about your path. Growth requires both the acquisition and application of knowledge. Before I discovered Wealth Dynamics, I was trying to do everything myself. I'm a Creator, so I tended to live with my head in the realms of infinite possibility. But then I'd get frustrated with the more grounded, administrative "stuff." I was constantly fighting battles with myself in my own business. I knew I was only as strong as my weakest link, so instead of focusing on my strengths, I constantly addressed my weaknesses.

Wealth Dynamics helped me to understand and avoid these conflicts. It taught me that if I don't enjoy number-crunching, I shouldn't do it. I realized that not only could I focus on just what I enjoyed doing, but that it was an absolute necessity in order to achieve what I wanted to achieve. Every time I did something not true to my profile, I created conflict and endangered the future of my business. The way to transcend this conflict was to stick to my area of greatest contribution.

Wealth Dynamics has been a great catalyst in my own development. Four years ago, I wrote a vision of what I wished my future to be. Today, about eighty percent of my vision has come to pass. I do what I love and love what I do, am building more wealth than ever before and I travel the world and work with others from over thirty countries to create a brighter future. I know that I am on the path that's right for me.

In my business, Tenkai, we guide others to find their individual and organizational path — and adapt to a congruent life in line with their purpose. Tenkai means, "change for the better." Similarly, Wealth Dynamics encourages people to find their purpose, and acts as a road map that allows people to serve that purpose in the most effective way for them.

For instance, one of my clients, Auriel Blanche, wrote a children's book intended to help her niece overcome some typical childhood problems. When we first met, sixteen years after the book was written, she had not managed to get it published. Last year she finally succeeded. Now she can share her message effectively, and move forward with her vision of children helping other children around the world. She just needed to find her way in order to make her vision a reality.

As with martial arts, Wealth Dynamics is built on core principles. Once you've learned the core principles of Wealth Dynamics and discovered your profile, you can use that understanding to find your own way.

Auriel had created a wonderful gift for the present that had the power to change the future, but she hadn't given it to the world. Only by giving this gift would its potential be fully realized. By not publishing the book, she was not honoring her purpose (an all-too-common affliction in our society). I used Wealth Dynamics to help her understand that what she was doing was characteristic of her Creator profile. Creators typically start something great, only to have great difficulty in taking it to its full potential.

As with martial arts, Wealth Dynamics is built on core principles. Once you've learned the core principles of Wealth Dynamics and discovered your profile, you can use that understanding to find your own way. The most powerful models, such as Wealth Dynamics, explain the past and guide your action in the present to create the future. When you consider how a principle applies to your past experiences, it not only provides you with a greater depth of understanding; it actually results in integration of the knowledge. The beauty of integrated knowledge is that it is applied without conscious thought. That is the essence of true growth.

When we gain further knowledge and move to a greater level of awareness, we can sometimes suffer from a kind of intellectual paralysis. There are so many actions we can take that we end up not acting at all. Inspired to create massive change, we may become overwhelmed by the tremendous future possibilities for ourselves and others — and then never take the first step on the journey. The solution to this is simple: just identify the first three steps to take.

The first thing to do is to get into flow. All of us have had the feeling of being in flow, inspired, energized and completely present in the moment, and it is important to get reacquainted with that feeling for reference. Next, identify your path, your way. If you are on the wrong path, everything will be increasingly difficult. Third, just go and do something in line with your purpose. Anything, however small, that creates a positive change. The best way to change the world is one step at a time.

When you start doing more things in line with your purpose, you feel energized. You get inspired, which in turn enables you to do more, accomplish more. We often grow without even realizing it. I like to tell of a young man who mastered the art of the sword. He spent years practicing, totally focused on sharpening his skill with his sword. One day, his sword was taken away, and he was confronted with a great challenge. At that point, the value of all he had learned was really tested. Following the test, he realized that he had integrated the principles of his art; he had discovered that his power did not lie in the sword, it lay within. Mastery of the sword brought about mastery of the self.

People so often associate their worth with things outside of themselves. It is not about the sword, your job, your qualifications or your assets. It is about your core principles, your personal center, where your spirit and true value lie. In our current economic climate, we are fortunate to face circumstances that challenge our attachments. I hope that this "crisis" leaves us with a world full of people who recognize and leverage their true value, twenty-first-century samurai who know their purpose, the one worth really living for.

Andy Greenhill is an international business consultant, founder of Tenkai Consulting, Ltd., and a traditional martial artist. He is a sought-after speaker whose "Enduring Enterprise" framework empowers businesses to thrive in the new economy. Andy has successfully integrated the practical insights of the West with the timeless wisdom of the East, identifying the core principles of enduring success. Presenting these with unique clarity and precision, he helps leaders discover the hidden potential within themselves and their organizations, charting their path to excellence. To learn more about Andy and his work, please visit www.tenkai.co.uk.

Successful Communication
Begins with a Shift
in Perception

BERNADETTE WILLEMS

The heart of all relationships is communication. That may sound trite, but that is because it is so unfailingly true. Since I hear the phrase so often, I assume everyone knows how true it is — and yet I am constantly amazed by how often poor communication ruins a relationship, personal or professional. I am especially amazed and saddened to see poor communication destroy a marriage.

For years, I witnessed an untold number of acrimonious divorce cases in which husbands and wives did not talk with each other, but instead used lawyers as mouthpieces to viciously tear at each other, all in order to "win." It never ceased to astonish me that people who had once been so in love could inspire such venom in each other. The fights were even more horrible when children were involved.

For a long time, I knew there must be some other way, some alternative to these pointless battles. I believed that conflict is self-destructive and damaging to anyone involved — individuals, families, organizations. And I felt that with the right approach, much of the damage could be avoided. What is more, after long and protracted court battles, all to render "winning" verdicts, I could not escape the conclusion that nobody — except the well-paid lawyers — had won anything. There has to be a better way, I kept thinking. And finally, fifteen years ago, I was introduced to that better way: mediation. Mediation provides win-win solutions in conflicts and disputes, whereas the outcome of litigation is uncertain, and often both parties end up losing.

I trained as a mediator fifteen years ago. At the time, I was the only mediator in my then legal firm, Simon Bergin, where I was a partner. In 1996, my firm was the first in Greater Manchester to be involved in the LSC Mediation Pilot Scheme, and subsequently to receive a franchise to mediate in family matters. Today, I head a team of experienced lawyer-mediators who work with me to resolve disputes in family, contact and divorce matters, as well as workplace and commercial disputes. In mediation, I help my clients achieve resolutions to their disputes in a way that will help them make sense of their own lives, save substantial sums of money and preserve important relationships. It is staggering how much money you can save by avoiding a protracted and adversarial legal process.

The key to mediation is communication. Oftentimes, when people are fighting, they cannot communicate because they simply do not hear each other. In a dispute, two people can be saying the same thing, but in completely different ways — so they do not even realize they are in agreement. What I am skilled at is identifying what people want — and explaining it to all parties involved, so each person trusts that I have her best interests in mind.

Mediation provides win-win solutions in conflicts and disputes, whereas the outcome of litigation is uncertain, and often both parties end up losing.

For instance, I once worked with an incredibly acrimonious couple. In the meeting, they were very hostile to each other, and very animated and agitated. Fighting over what would happen to their children, they talked at each other in a way that made it impossible for them to listen to or hear each other. They were not even listening to me. I wondered how best to deal with the situation.

I decided to write down everything they were saying on a flip chart. Then I sat down and said nothing. This caught their attention. I pointed out to them what I had written: "There's your agreement," I said. They both looked at the chart and, to my surprise, they laughed, suddenly realizing they had actually been in synch. Through the mediation process, they identified what they wanted and sorted out how they would achieve it. A successful mediation leaves people feeling better than they would after a successful day in court, because they have learned how to listen and communicate better, and come away with valuable relationship tools.

Since encountering Wealth Dynamics, I am quicker and more efficient at dealing with my clients — a cost benefit to them and a time benefit to me.

Before encountering Wealth Dynamics, I was operating a successful mediation practice, but I was aware that some aspects of running my business did not come easily to me; they seemed laborious and tedious and did not provide me with the job satisfaction I felt while mediating.

Now that I know my profile, I understand why I love helping clients find better ways of resolving their disputes. Knowing my Wealth Dynamics profile has also helped me determine the level of support I need in my business to achieve that sense of always being "in flow."

Finding my "natural game" has helped me identify other dynamics that operate in relationships, and provided me with additional skills which have proven to be very useful. Wealth Dynamics has helped me to unravel what makes people behave the way they do. Since encountering Wealth Dynamics, I am quicker and more efficient at dealing with my clients — a cost benefit to them and a time benefit to me.

When I am mediating a family dispute, such as a divorce case, I use Wealth Dynamics discreetly. If I am with someone who is outgoing and someone who is an introvert, a Star and a Mechanic, for example, and I spot those differences, I am able to identify potential conflicts in their approaches to the process. I do not explain their Wealth Dynamics profiles to my clients, but I do use their profiles to mediate.

Not all divorce cases are strictly about the divorce. Many times they also involve children. Four years ago I trained in direct consultation with children. This means that, with the joint agreement of the parents, I can meet with a child in private and listen to him. Our meetings are confidential, and if the child wants any of the conversation reported to his parents, I do so in a sensitive manner. This process helps a child be heard, and also offers the child the support of the mediator. It is a very powerful way to break impasse situations in contact cases, even though no responsibility is given to the child to decide the outcome.

I do not find it particularly necessary or useful to establish Wealth Dynamics profiles with children. I will, however, often use formal profiling in workplace mediations. Many of my commercial mediations involve private organizations, and my experience has been that most of the organizations regret my not being called in sooner. Most organizations do not have mediation policies, and they should. And most organizations do not address mediation soon enough.

I also mediate in the public sector. For instance, I was recently hired to manage a dispute among social workers who assisted the elderly and physically handicapped. These social workers were dispatched, as teams, to various communities where they helped their clients in many ways, including through the promotion of physical exercise.

Most organizations do not have mediation policies, and they should. And most organizations do not address mediation soon enough.

Since these social workers were great with their clients, they were promoted to management levels. None of them were trained as managers, however, so they were not effective. Then, if a team member went on maternity leave, or was switched to another unit, the problems — and the stress — grew. They were all at the ends of their tethers by the time I came in.

I gave them time to voice their grievances and listen to each other. Then I drew them out, asking what they were good at, what their strengths were, when they found things easy. I asked these questions to discern when they each were in their flow. Then I asked questions to get them to discover the gaps in themselves and their unit. In answering my questions, they discovered how to resolve their problems. My job was to help them unearth their own solutions through the questions I asked.

I have found that the biggest barrier to resolving disputes with dignity is a lack of understanding on the part of one party. For instance, a client may come to me because he wants to divorce his wife, which indicates he has done a lot of thinking about it. And yet, as is often the case, his wife had no clue her husband was considering divorce. Naturally, she is quite surprised. She had no idea the marriage was not working, because her husband never communicated as much.

The problem with this scenario, then, is that the two sides perceive things differently. In mediation, it is my job to explain to them that the husband may see the car (the issues) as white, and the wife may see the car (the issues) as black, but that is because they are standing on different sides of the street. The issues are the same, but their individual perceptions and reactions may be very different. When they recognize and acknowledge this, they can move on.

Wealth Dynamics has greatly enhanced my ability to illustrate to clients the difference in their perceptions. A simple shift in awareness breaks down barriers to communication in any relationship — it works with couples, corporations and teams of every kind. To view the whole car — the whole picture — frees people from their misconceptions and assumptions, and allows for successful resolutions to any conflict.

Bernadette Willems is an experienced family solicitor and mediator, and is a Director of Greater Manchester Mediation Limited. She is a member of several professional organizations, including Family Mediation Association; Family Mediation Council; College of Mediators; Association of High Achievers; ADR and Law Society. Bernadette has contributed to several European and international conferences. Bernadette also specializes in mediation training and Everything DiSC to help organizations enhance their sales, management and conflict resolution to improve their bottom line. She is a coach, and a Master Practitioner in NLP, and is fluent in both French and English.

Trusting Your Instincts: Your Natural Game

DEB MAYBURY

Years ago I came to the realization that martial arts and self-defense encompass more than a technique, a kick or a punch. They are about self-awareness — mental and physical. They are guided by natural instincts and flow.

In 1973, I watched a movie called Enter the Dragon starring Bruce Lee. From that evening forward, and up until February of 1993, I held, yet suppressed, a desire to "try" Kung Fu. Finally, the longevity and constancy of my pull toward martial arts indicated to me that — just maybe — I should stop procrastinating, research local schools and seek out what would turn into a life-changing experience.

From the very first class, twenty years after the first seed was planted, I loved it. Everything — the moves, the discipline, the camaraderie, the instructor and particularly the deep sense of calm it unexpectedly gave me. I had not anticipated that Kung Fu, a physical activity, would bring peacefulness to my life, as well as an understanding of myself I had not previously experienced.

Interestingly enough, my friends did not enthusiastically receive my training stories. No one I spoke to identified with my new passion, or understood why I would expose myself to the rigors of training. "You're paranoid." "Why don't you just buy a gun?" they teased. "Why would you like doing that?" Their questions were posed as if there was something wrong with either it or me. I find it interesting that I love traveling, writing, hockey and Yorkshire terriers too — but nobody asks why I love those things.

Too often, we ignore internal messages. We are led down paths by parents, peers and employers that are not safe or best suited for us. Ironically, we often make these choices either because we disregard our own safety or because we fear for our security. Be true to yourself, do more of what YOU love.

Who knows why we love what we love? We just do. I've continued to experiment in many disciplines including Kung Fu, Karate, boxing, kickboxing, grappling, Taekwondo, Wing Chun and Commando Krav Maga because my mind, body and spirit love the challenge, and I hold an appreciation for all that these various styles have to offer. At forty-seven, I am pleased that I still surprise myself — and my younger peers — with what I can do. Physical endurance, strength, coordination and mindfulness are all elements within this journey.

Be true to yourself, do more of what YOU love.

I created Realistic Self-Defense For Women (RSD) because I felt — and still feel — strongly that it is my purpose to share what I have learned over the years. My system is different from most because it is designed for women by a woman. I accelerate students' learning by teaching them to use their natural reflexes and to combine easy-to-learn mental strategies and physical techniques while focusing on their strengths versus another's weaknesses.

RSD is largely about empowering women to make wise decisions and be prepared, not paranoid. It is critical to pay attention to our intuition and be more cognizant of red flags in situations and relationships. In self-protection, avoiding a bad situation in the first place is much easier than trying to get out of something that is unfolding around you. For me personally, teaching is about helping each student accentuate her natural movements and honor her abilities, talents and flow.

Awareness and illumination of strengths are keys to being successful in both self-protection and Wealth Dynamics. You have a natural path. There are things you do better than others without even trying. We often spend a lifetime trying to be good at what we were never meant to do, then wonder why we are unsatisfied. Wealth Dynamics teaches individuals how to find and follow their path of least resistance.

All my life I've received clues to what I should be doing. As a child, I always had several projects underway. Sculpting, drawing, painting, sports, playing guitar, writing songs and poems — at fourteen, I recall buying a blank journal with the intention of writing a book.

Thirty years later, I discovered Wealth Dynamics. Taking the Wealth Dynamics profile test was the moment of enlightenment, when I realized what I was meant to do. "This means I should write!" I thought. Writing had always put me in my flow. Clues to your path of least resistance lie within your passion for, your flow within, and your enjoyment of, an activity. We should do more of what gets us to jump out of bed in the morning.

After this enlightening moment, I sat down at my desk and wrote the first pages of a book I had wanted to write for a long time. Creators are not always good finishers, so I motivated myself by holding an image in my mind of a young girl who had asked a lot of questions in a self-protection class I'd taught at a local high school. She was afraid of the dark, afraid of strangers — afraid of too many things.

I wanted to reassure her that she didn't need to be so afraid, while providing her with tools to move through her fear and become stronger and more confident. I also wanted to learn more about what other teenage girls were afraid of. This one girl's willingness to express her fears inspired me to write for many other girls and their parents and make them aware that they are not alone.

Clues to your path of least resistance lie within your passion for, your flow within, and your enjoyment of, an activity. We should do more of what gets us to jump out of bed in the morning.

I had not realized, before compiling my survey results, that so many girls are living with so much fear. They are not just afraid of an attack; they're afraid of social pressure, ostracism, expressing themselves, falling short of parental expectations, the future and more. Concerned that their worries would prevent them from exploring, taking chances and being true to who they are, I also wrote to offer them some realistic, empowering ways to work through those fears. Writing was very exciting. The more I wrote, the faster the words flowed. Keeping in mind, though, that Creators are not generally great with details, I knew the birthing of my project would soon need a support team behind it, a group of people with natural abilities to do the things that I do not do well.

It was a great relief when the team naturally came together. My cohorts took care of the essentials I wasn't any good at and didn't enjoy. I asked for help when I needed it, and delegated tasks such as collecting data and reference material. In the past I would have been frustrated by these tasks, while still feeling that I had to complete them myself. Now my team freed me up to follow my path of least resistance. What a relief to have permission and direction to do what I wanted to do — write! I did not need to do it all.

I am thankful for being introduced to Wealth Dynamics profiling, because it deepened my understanding of my strengths and weaknesses: my Dynamo energy, intuitiveness, vision, optimism and ability to initiate exciting new projects — as well as my tendency to burn others out, get distracted and have too many things going on at once. With this knowledge, for the first time, I allowed myself the freedom to sit down and write.

Within about four months, working part-time, I had accomplished what I'd always dreamed of: I'd finished the first draft of my book, *What Is Your Teenage Daughter Afraid Of?* The book was self-published a couple of months later.

Wealth Dynamics also helped me realize that in following my heart, my natural game and my passions, I would find real wealth. Being a Master Practitioner of Wealth Dynamics is the perfect complement to the work I was already doing helping women and girls harness their inner strength and understand their natural flow. Currently, I merge Wealth Dynamics with Realistic Self-Defense when I speak at corporations and high schools.

There is a natural path to wealth for each of us; what we must do to find it is get in flow with our natural game. Using my education in Wealth Dynamics, my Realistic Self-Defense business grew more than fifty percent last fall. I have also co-created an additional business, Discover Wealth Dynamics, and encountered many joint-venture opportunities with like-minded individuals bringing different talents, passions and skills to the table.

Perhaps best of all, What Is Your Teenage Daughter Afraid Of? is now in the hands of hundreds of girls. Last year I mentioned that I was seeking sponsors so I could give each of my students a copy of my book. An amazing Lord profile colleague provided the funds to distribute three hundred copies of it to three different high schools.

As we must trust our instincts in order to protect ourselves from physical danger, we must also trust our instincts — our natural game — in order to live a rich, satisfying and joyful life.

Deb Maybury is currently re-creating herself mentally and physically as she prepares to cycle across Canada to raise awareness and funds for children with and beyond cancer. She is the owner of Dradalm Promotions, a personal fitness trainer and the creator of Realistic Self-Defense For Women (see www.RealisticsSelfDefenseforWomen.com). Deb is a Black Sash in Kung Fu and a Black Belt in Karate. She is a Master Practitioner of Wealth Dynamics and the co-creator of Discover Wealth Dynamics (www.DiscoverWealthDynamics.com). She is also the author of the book What Is Your Teenage Daughter Afraid Of?

Sustainable Success through Cyclical Awareness

SHERI GREENWELL

The only constant in life is change. The world continually moves in and out of seasons, countries continue to usher in new leadership and organizations grow. Change is required to grow as person, in a relationship and in a business, yet so often we resist it under the guise of maintaining stability. Sustainable growth is possible when we are mindful of the seasons; looking ahead to the next phase of development, we not only ensure our survival — we thrive. In more than twenty-five years helping organizations identify opportunities, shift focus and develop systems to support growth, I have seen many companies transform by embracing the cyclical nature of business.

Wealth Dynamics correlates these cycles of business to the four seasons in nature. Spring is a time for beginnings — launching businesses, initiating new projects, starting relationships. It is a time of unknowns, but also a time for innovating, creating products and markets, developing ideas and proving concepts. In Summer, the focus is on building momentum, expanding reach and growing markets. A business gains its core operating team and footing during this season, and from that foundation is able to blaze away and consolidate its ability to deliver on brand promises. In a company's Autumn phase, work becomes automatic and the business starts to see the real fruits of its labors. With the business firmly established, sales come easily, and attention shifts to retaining and nurturing customers. Winter necessitates concentration on properly stewarding the harvest, and steadying the company for the next cycle.

It is a natural time to focus on optimizing cash flow and perfecting systems in preparation for the inevitable oncoming Spring.

Think back to the last time you started a new job. The first six-month period is all new — full of uncertainty, promise and excitement (Spring). Then you get your bearings, get to know people and learn how to function in the job (Summer). After a couple of years, you know the ropes and have established your position in the company (Autumn). Eventually you are in a set routine, holding steady and, one hopes, exploring ways to improve policies, procedures and systems (Winter).

Sustained, long-term success depends on awareness of seasonality in business.

In my experience, people often get stuck in Winter. They fall into a rut, unable to start the cycle over again. This causes people to feel cynical about their work, or turn in a lackluster performance. It happens with entrepreneurs, management and CEOs, too. Some leaders are so focused on maintaining the stability of their company that they end up driving it to an inevitable collapse.

Sustained, long-term success depends on awareness of seasonality in business. Just look at the history of the top companies in any field, powerhouses that have weathered economic downturns, technological advances and fierce competition. Whether they consciously mirrored the four seasons in their strategic planning and implementation or called it something else entirely, the leaders of many industry giants were aware of the cyclical nature of business, and acted accordingly.

Take Kodak, for example, a company that invented, cornered and continuously redefined the market for photographic film. Founded in 1881 by George Eastman and his investor, Henry A. Strong, Kodak began as the Eastman Dry Plate Company, manufacturing photographic plates for cameras. A bank clerk, Eastman fell in love with photography but found the process of taking and developing pictures complicated, messy and cumbersome. After three years of late nights experimenting in his mother's kitchen, Eastman invented a dry photographic plate formula and a machine to produce the plates in large quantities. Patent in hand, Eastman set up shop with the goal of selling his plates to photographers.

In his company's first Spring, Eastman developed a proven concept and introduced the product to the marketplace. Moving into Summer, he directed his attention to building his market. He invested in advertising, focused on producing a quality product, and quickly became a leader in the industry. As the company entered Autumn, Eastman shifted his focus to maintaining customers. During this time, his steadfast commitment to them was tested when a batch of plates went bad. He spent his "last dollar" recalling the defective product, but he ultimately saved the company's reputation. During the first Winter of the Eastman Dry Plate Company, Eastman formulated a plan to streamline systems and improve production.

Eastman continued to experiment, inventing the first photographic film in 1883.

If George Eastman had continued to focus solely on manufacturing photographic plates, and on selling to hobbyists and professional photographers, he might well have gone out of business within a few years. But Eastman seemed to have an innate knowledge of the cyclical nature of business. So he brought a new Spring to the company that would soon revolutionize photography. Eastman continued to experiment, inventing the first photographic film in 1883.

At the end of this new season, however, he realized that many photographers were continuing to use plates despite the convenience of film. So he entered a new Spring, and set a goal of making the "camera as convenient as the pencil." Eastman developed the first Kodak camera in 1888, effectively forming a new, mass market for his company. A natural innovator, and quite probably a Creator profile, Eastman revitalized his company over and over again through cycles of seasons. He never got stuck in the stagnancy of Winter. Formally established as Eastman Kodak in 1895, Eastman's company would go on creating new markets through the invention of new products: x-ray image capture, microfilm, film and chemicals for the motion picture industry — and, in 1936, Kodachrome, the first 35mm color film.

In the digital age, decades after George Eastman passed away, Kodak continues to thrive through innovation. Ironically, it was a Kodak engineer who invented the first digital camera in 1975, which eventually led to the discontinuation of Kodak film cameras. Rather than staying in Winter, trying to hang on to old ways and outdated products, the company changed its focus again, and concentrated on supplying printing papers for home use, self-serve photo-printing kiosks and other digital photo innovations.

Kodak is a success story because, from the very beginning, it worked through the cycles appropriately. Utilizing Wealth Dynamics profiling enables businesses to move through the seasons even more effectively, potentially achieving equally dynamic results. Entrepreneurial leadership works well in the beginning, but it can be destabilizing as the company progresses through the cycles. If you don't recognize that things are changing and match your business leadership to the season accordingly, your business could go into decline.

When a person with the wrong profile for the current business season manages a company, it's like driving with the brakes on.

When a person with the wrong profile for the current business season manages a company, it's like driving with the brakes on. For example, during a company's Spring cycle, when the goal is to develop and promote concepts, Creators and Stars would be the natural leaders. However, at some point they will have to hand over the reins to someone who can build and consolidate. In Summer, when companies need to build markets and networks, Deal Makers and Supporters would be appropriate leaders. As companies move into the Autumn cycle of welcoming and servicing customers, Traders and Accumulators should move into leadership roles.

In Winter, when everything is settled and the focus is on building and consolidating systems, the company would benefit most from the guidance of Lords and Mechanics. While the Wealth Dynamics model is excellent, building systems at the end of the cycle can cause chaos very quickly and impede growth. I have found that putting in a little bit of flexible structure right from the beginning supports effective growth. It's a balance — if you have endless creation you will have dissipation; if you have too much focus on systems you will squeeze the life out of your business.

Albert Einstein said, "The significant problems we face cannot be solved at the same level of thinking we were at when we created them." Rather than set someone up to be a manager in all seasons, consider employing cyclical leadership. This is a radical concept, and you would need a tight, aligned team with shared values and purpose to make it work. Yet when different profiles play different roles on a team, each assuming the lead position when seasonally appropriate, the possibilities are limitless.

There is seasonality to all things — to relationships with parents, children, and partners; to careers, political movements, the evolution of cultures. The challenge is to have enough foresight to be aware of the impending seasons and adapt to the cycles. When you move through the seasons with intent, shifting focus and leadership accordingly, your endeavors will always be in flow. And, like Kodak, your company will rise to every challenge, innovating products, services or systems that we have yet to imagine.

Sheri Greenwell has over twenty-five years' experience in business in a wide range of roles in diverse industries. As director and principal consultant for EnQuantum Ltd., Sheri guides individuals, teams and businesses through the chaos of change. A popular speaker and sought-after facilitator, Sheri has a knack for spotting improvement opportunities before they turn into problems. She provides businesses with winning solutions responsive to holistic organizational needs, building effective teams and providing leadership and innovative approaches to the development of company culture.

Sheri holds a BS in chemistry and general business from Saginaw Valley State University and is a Master Practitioner of neuro-linguistic programming (NLP). She has trained extensively in Wealth Dynamics, Spiral Dynamics and AVI Values Inventory. Sheri is a member of the Human Resources Institute of New Zealand (HRINZ), the New Zealand Association for Training and Development (NZATD), the New Zealand Institute of Safety Management (NZISM) and the XL Results Foundation, an international network of entrepreneurs. To learn more about Sheri, visit www.SheriGreenwell.com.

Layers of Discovery

MARK CRAIG

To me, one of the most fascinating aspects of life is that nothing is ever just black or white. Everything worth deep exploration is so because it is layered, nuanced. Peel back a layer and you find another to explore. For the curious mind, this isn't frustrating; it's exciting. Perhaps that's why, several years ago, after a successful career as a clinical pharmacist and educator within in the UK hospital system, I decided it was high time I got out of the traditional 9 to 5 and did something new and exciting. I had always enjoyed the many interactive layers of my job. I was a clinician; an educator, teaching doctors and other healthcare professionals; and an advocate, interfacing between health care providers and patients to determine which approaches would best suit patients' health issues and personal lives. But as time went on, I found myself doing less interacting and more paperwork. It was time to make a change. So I went out on a limb.

In October of 2006, I left my job. I didn't have specific guidance about my decision — it just felt right. I studied and began practicing hypnotherapy. Then I began teaching again, and coaching. The variety in my professional work re-infused me with enthusiasm. I loved speaking to and working with others. I loved working for a month and taking a month off to see the world. I felt fulfilled. Still, I questioned myself: "Am I doing the right thing?"

I didn't have the language for what was so right about my decision — and my persistent self-examination — until I met a group of social entrepreneurs through XL and was introduced to Wealth Dynamics. A friend invited me to visit Las Vegas, and I signed up for a Wealth Dynamics weekend there. What happened during that workshop changed my life. And just three weeks later, I found myself attending a Master Practitioner workshop in Bali. I hadn't planned for it, but I knew I couldn't miss it.

When I learned that I was a Supporter profile with secondary Star/Deal Maker activation, the layers of my life choices made sense to me, and I was able to fully embrace them. Through Wealth Dynamics, I recognized myself: my desire to support and communicate with others. My need for variety and travel. My interest and education in many forms of medicine. My lack of enthusiasm for marketing myself and following through. My constant self-examination. (Supporter profiles can be a bit like Alice in Wonderland, always looking at alternatives and wondering which to pursue.) All these are characteristics of my primary and secondary profiles.

I had always been excited about personality and profiling systems, fascinated by the shifting layers of persona within human beings — what makes them tick, what makes them click together in personal and professional relationships. Wealth Dynamics, with its grounding in the ancient I Ching and the cyclical nature of the seasons of the earth, offered me a nuanced system in which to explore these questions.

When I learned that I was a Supporter profile with secondary Star/Deal Maker activation, the layers of my life choices made sense to me, and I was able to fully embrace them.

Recognizing myself as a Supporter taught me many things. One of them was to let go of my traditional idea of what an entrepreneur is supposed to be: a go-it-alone pioneer. Instead, I saw that entrepreneurs may begin alone, but it's when they create teams of complementary profiles that their ventures really begin to take off and flow. No one person can do it all. And I saw that, as a Supporter, it's more than okay for me to be an entrepreneur within someone else's business, not just my own, just as it's okay to form long-term partnerships or strategic alliances and collaborations with entrepreneurs of other energies. There are layers of entrepreneurship to be discovered, not just the old maverick construct that's based on a competitive approach to business.

So not only does Wealth Dynamics embrace a whole series of layers within individuals based on their primary and secondary profiles and seasonal energies; it is also all about effectively layering the skills and attributes of these individuals within groups, and, according to where a business is seasonally located, to make dynamic, healthy wholes. This fits right in with what I've always believed is possible in the medical field.

Each of the profiles, for instance, has eight different potential interactions. How a Supporter interacts with a Creator, a Lord, another Supporter, etc., is very different from how a Lord will communicate. Eight times eight makes sixty-four possibilities for communication. We call this system the "64 vectors." That's a lot of layers of possibility in human interaction, a lot of opportunity, which is one of the main ideas I like to open for my coaching and facilitating clients.

There are layers of entrepreneurship to be discovered, not just the old maverick construct that's based on a competitive approach to business.

I was coaching a client who had just left full-time employment to start up her own business. As we determined the best structure for her role in the business, I picked up on her language patterns, which were, at surface level, highly suggestive of Supporter/Blaze energy. Peeling away further, I considered how much time she spent speaking, and how much listening. (These are just two layers to look at when considering profile and communication.) Though my client needed and enjoyed having other profiles around her in the workplace, she recognized that it was easiest and most satisfying for her to communicate with other Supporters, and she noticed ways in which the conversation was different when discussing certain business matters with other profiles. She also realized what duties she needed to contract out to others, such as marketing, so that she could avoid frustration and do what she loved to do and did best.

Studying the 64-vector structure — taking into account the Dynamo, Blaze, Earth and Metal energies — we see that though Wealth Dynamics acknowledges the many layers inherent in humans and nature at large, it's still a simple way to understand how people work, and how they'll best collaborate. Fresh starts are best in spring. Reaping great benefits is natural to fall. Creators need the Blaze, Tempo and Steel frequencies that Supporters and Accumulators provide. Traders need Dynamo, Blaze and Steel energy from Lord and Star profiles. When we see our many-layered connections, we see that we all need each other. Because Wealth Dynamics is based on simply paying attention to the cycles of nature and acknowledging and appreciating the way we are, it never fails.

As a Supporter, I have a teaching and coaching style that is all about inclusion and being highly interactive. I access my Star energy in order to shine in front of a group, but in my own Supporter fashion. Now, when I teach or facilitate for a corporate group, I notice how different profiles ask questions either during or after our time together. I use my background in Wealth Dynamics to make sure I can reach everyone, and we can all enjoy discovery as a group. It's really fascinating. Creators ask very short, to-the-point questions, interested in short answers and visual examples. Accumulators and Lords will ask much more detailed questions, usually about scientific research and requiring more auditory and detailed answers and written guidelines. The Supporters are usually just happy to ask me a question later on after our workshop, in an informal setting like a coffee shop or bar.

> *Because Wealth Dynamics is based on simply paying attention to the cycles of nature and acknowledging and appreciating the way we are, it never fails.*

Another amazing thing is, Wealth Dynamics is a uniquely international language. Living in the UK and having traveled all over the world and spoken with people from many cultures and countries, I've found that no matter what our primary languages are, no matter our nationalities and backgrounds, Wealth Dynamics and its insights translate universally into the two core elements of relationships and finance.

Being in flow for me as a Supporter feels like play. Play requires imagination and discovery. Uncovering layer after layer within myself, within my business and in the world at large — and helping others to do the same — has become my purpose, and an unending source of tremendous richness in my life.

Mark Craig is a top-tier performance coach and strategist, using his expertise to bring individuals, organizations and corporations new strategies for progress and success. Having been coached and mentored by some of the most well-known and respected coaches and mentors in the world, Mark incorporates his skills as a Master Practitioner of Wealth Dynamics, NLP (neuro-linguistic programming), and hypnotherapy to enhance his coaching practice. Mark's initial background is as a registered pharmacist with the Royal Pharmaceutical Society of Great Britain. Today, he combines this background with an expertise in holistic medicines, making him a highly experienced and sought after facilitator within the healthcare sector as well as a thriving corporate coach. For more information about Mark Craig, visit www.SimplyAskStrategies.com.

Visioning the "What"

MELINDA WOOLF

What if you could make your dreams come true outside the boundaries of time, space and money? I'm not talking about the reasonable and realistic, "do-able" dream; I'm talking about the dream — the one you talk about with anyone who will listen, the one that makes you feel whole, alive, inspired and on purpose. The one that fills you up inside! The vision for your life you've been carrying around in your heart, waiting, wishing, and wanting for the time to make it real.

Perhaps achieving your dreams without an endless supply of expendable cash and an abundance of free time sounds like a fairy tale, something that happens for other people, not for you. You may feel you'd have to employ some sort of magic spell to materialize that innovative product, to write your bestselling book or to start a transformational movement. Or you may feel that realizing your vision requires sacrifice, working tirelessly and going out and making it happen, forcing your dream into reality no matter what. Nothing could be further from the truth. There is an easier way! Simply be willing to look within and discover, awaken to and surrender completely into your divine flow.

In the past, I created solely through control and manifestation. Using my personal life force and energy field, I generated results by doing, physically barreling through until I achieved what I wanted. I micro-managed every detail along the way, from the imagination of the creative ideas and application to the financial, scheduling and legal requirements. You name it — I was on top of it. I was good at it, too.

As a producer and creator of advertising, television and films, I had a satisfying (and financially lucrative) career, and I led an interesting life. From a very young age, I traveled the globe for a series of top-level, high-stress jobs. From working as a creative producer in a successful commercial production company to managing a boutique ad agency in Los Angeles, my clients included American Express, Häagen-Dazs, United Airlines and Fox. I worked long hours making sure every project was just right for high-profile projects, such as the launches of Desperate Housewives, the American Express Blue Campaign and Spike TV, and the re-branding of ABC.

There is an easier way! Simply be willing to look within and discover, awaken to and surrender completely into your divine flow.

Everything was going along as planned. I was in control and on top of the world! Shortly after beginning a master's degree in spiritual psychology, I was presented with the opportunity to choose between two high-level executive job offers, one at a large television network, and another at a top ad agency. This triggered a period of introspection that changed my life completely. Suddenly I realized I was out of sync with myself and with what I was a part of creating professionally. I was no longer even reading the scripts for the projects I was producing. I was simply going through the motions, and I had stopped caring all together. And worse, I was not creating in integrity; instead, I was unconsciously churning out project after project, without consideration of the messages going out to audiences worldwide. I was creating media with little or no respect for how it could affect the way millions (and potentially billions) of people live their lives, what they think, how they spend their money and what they might assume as "truth." I had an "Aha!" moment that forever changed my life — for the better.

I recognized media as a profoundly powerful tool, and I made a declaration to the Universe: from this point forward I would ONLY create in service of inspiring, educating and empowering people. I made a fierce choice and took immediate action. I resigned from my position, turned down the other job offers and committed to creating media from my heart. And, to be clear that I was in integrity with myself in this commitment, I decided I would not profit from my projects for at least one year!

Very quickly I realized that not only could I complete projects with little or no money, just by letting go of the responsibility of making it happen all by myself, but I could also create media that inspired and enthralled me. I interviewed world leaders, showcased conscious businesses and shined light on many worthwhile projects and people doing GREAT things in service to humanity. With this I was primed to intuit and embrace the principles of Wealth Dynamics.

When I opened myself up to creating in flow, it was a blessed confirmation of what I have come to understand and love about me! My natural state of being is that of a Creator, and when I fully embrace this role, when I surrender to my flow and fully allow myself to imagine, vision, and receive the "What," in its greatest possible version, all of the resources, people and money show up naturally. Creating in universal flow begins with simply awakening to the type of question we are each individually naturally guided to answer. For every great idea that makes it out into the world and into our mainstream culture, there are countless genius ideas that are never realized, as projects and businesses stall when people try to answer the wrong question and/or try to do it all themselves, much like I did in the past.

I recognized media as a profoundly powerful tool, and I made a declaration to the Universe: from this point forward I would ONLY create in service of inspiring, educating and empowering people.

Wealth Dynamics taught me to ask the right questions and in the right order, so that the best ideas and most promising projects and businesses can come to fruition. For example, as a Creator profile, I always begin with the question "What." The natural sequence of flow begins with "What," then "Who," "When/Where," "How" and then "What" again. The "What" drives the "What," so to speak!

For some people, simply asking the right question enables them to accomplish something that never before seemed possible. For me, someone who has never experienced challenge in manifesting my dreams, the gift of focusing on the "What" allows me to do so effortlessly and in JOY, beyond the perceived limitations of time, space and money, beyond the shoulds and should-nots, without must-haves and must-dos, without struggle. Best of all, creating this way is fun and empowering for me and for everyone involved!

When I "vision," fully embracing and allowing the divine flow of the "What," I allow my entire being to swim freely in the imagination space of possibility. I envision the biggest, brightest, and most dynamic ideas I can imagine, and then I map my vision in order of the natural sequence and cycle of flow, the sacred geometry of creation and life. I envision the "What" in vivid and exponential detail: the specifics of design and functionality, the timeline, the user experience, the price point, how it will function, who it will help, serve, and inspire, what it looks, feels, and sounds like. I take an idea to the very brink of what I can imagine is possible. Then, I get out of the way and allow it to happen. When I learned to focus primarily on the "What" I tapped into my flow, and suddenly creating became an effortless, joyous, allowing experience. I am able to build teams around my vision, my "What"—teams made up of people much better suited to answer the "Who," "When/Where" and "How" questions.

There is one additional and very important piece to creating in universal flow: "This, or something better, in service to the greatest good of all concerned."

This is where Wealth Dynamics truly shines! My team steps in and answers the questions of "Who," "When/Where" and "How," seamlessly and successfully! Not only do my team members know the answers to these questions, doing so is their purpose, what turns each of them on in the same way that it is my purpose to answer the question of "What!" I trust and empower the people on my team to answer these questions in their own spectacular ways. Although this might sound like a fairy tale, I can assure you it works brilliantly, and effortlessly.

There is one additional and very important piece to creating in universal flow: "This, or something better, in service to the greatest good of all concerned."

No matter how phenomenal the "What" I may vision is, I know there is always something better. There is always something brighter and more expansive. There is always something simpler, more usable, more dynamic. Knowing this is liberating, as it allows me to simply choose to enjoy myself, to literally be "in Joy" as I imagine, expand and allow the free flow of ideas to move to and through me.

Now I am free to co-create in abundance. A peace-centered educational program that works with youth in conjunction with the United Nations and International Peace Day; a global marketplace and community for conscious and innovative products, services and businesses; a global platform for conscious media — these are all a part of my vision and dream, and they are all a reality! Imagined and launched within three years' time. There are many other pieces, too many to count, that have come into fruition with minimal financial investment on my part. Of course it is helpful to have an expendable flow of available cash and currency, but the truth is that ideas are currency, time is currency, people and their talents are an even more valuable currency, and when we choose to leverage everything we have available to us, in service to our vision, our dreams, our "What," we do not specifically need money to make our dreams come true.

Awakening to our personal "What." This is the beginning of the dream. My greatest "What" is that together we realize a peace-centered world. Now that you know you can make your dreams come true beyond the boundaries of time and space, and even money, what will you choose to envision? What will you choose to create in service to our world? What is your greatest "What?"

Melinda Woolf is an independent filmmaker, a producer and creator of television programming and advertising, a brand consultant, author, speaker and facilitator. Melinda's gift as a visual storyteller is her ability to facilitate and translate the many multidimensional languages of the universe into comprehensive, and actionable communication through media, including: books, television, films, radio, technology, writing, teaching, and speaking.

Melinda is the CEO and co-founder of Conscious Innovations™ and Sa-

madhi Living™ Spa and Wellness Centers, (www.SamadhiLiving.com) as well as the founder and creator of Peace Centered™ (www.PeaceCentered.org), Vision Talk Radio™ (www.VisionTalkRadio.com) and Peace Centered TV™. President of the Dallas Chapter of the Women's National Book Association, Melinda is the author of The Abundance Mastery Course, (www.AbundanceCentered.com) and the Peace Centered curriculum. Connect with Melinda at www.Conscious -Innovations.com and www.IAmSoulCentered.com.

All Healing
Is Self-Healing

ELIZABETH REVELEY

Radical self care is the firm commitment to heal, beginning with oneself. It is the promise to be all you can be in every moment. It means living and loving with passion, remembering who you are and why you are here. When you practice radical self care, you are infusing yourself into your life with your undivided attention. Here's the payoff: The more conscious attention you pay to yourself and your activities, the more the real you is reflected in your actions and your life.

Radical self care is physical, emotional, mental and energetic alignment; every feeling you have, every thought you have, and how you direct your spirit is vital. If "Love is all there is," then our greatest personal practice is to breathe away everything else and come into alignment with our joy, our mastery — and our unconditional loving to fully express our unlimited selves. Whether you know it or not, you are developing the strength, stamina and flexibility of your Love and your Chi all the time. Love transforms the physical plane. It is all LOVE.

This is what I know about radical self care and love NOW, and I know that Wealth Dynamics dovetails perfectly with radical self care, but I didn't always know these things. It was all a journey taken step by beautiful step, each step taken with great trust. The longest journey begins with the first step, and life for me is a dance of steps and leaps, a continuous enlightening adventure. My Wealth Dynamics profile is Creator/Mechanic, and one of my gifts is to make things simple and clear so that more people can understand and incorporate offered wisdom into their lives. I am an action-oriented person. I love knowledge, and learning is fun, but knowledge is useless if you don't incorporate it into your life. Putting knowledge into action is a critical step. That's the step I was taking when I opened my school.

In 1984, I opened The American Institute of Massage Therapy in Kailua, Hawaii. It was a fledgling massage school in a small beach town, with incredible students from all over the world. Some arrived not knowing exactly why; they just knew they needed to be there, that there was something important for them to discover. Our website magnetized people from all over the world: we called it "magical marketing."

Breathtaking synergy occurs when you are living your passion and choose to put yourself in the midst of other bright, capable, passionate people. Life experience taught me that, and Wealth Dynamics reaffirmed it.

Day by day, for twenty years, I developed an extraordinary curriculum for massage therapy training and spiritual healing, spending each day doing what I loved. I had no business plan, and I had no exit strategy. It all came about because of my innate ability and conscious desire to collaborate. I followed my intuition, designed the foundational matrix and attracted the right people. I didn't realize it, but I was practicing Wealth Dynamics, which is partly why it resonated so much with me when I encountered it years later. Breathtaking synergy occurs when you are living your passion and you choose to put yourself in the midst of other bright, capable, passionate people. Life experience taught me that, and Wealth Dynamics reaffirmed it.

The foundation for the curriculum I designed and developed became known as Radical Self Care, officially named in 1996. The idea hit me when I was with my students sharing seated massage at an event for the Honolulu Fire Department. We were on a cement deck in downtown Honolulu, and as I watched everyone enjoy their massages, an intuitive knowing about the importance of self-care for everyone flooded over me. From that moment on, Radical Self Care became my mission.

Your personal practice is your responsibility on the path to self-mastery. Every action, every feeling, thought and communion with spirit emits a resonance and an attraction.

The basic components of Radical Self Care begin with what I call, "Life and Breath," because it promotes the three basic elements of life: Breath, Water and Gratitude — Breath because you might survive four minutes without breathing; Water because you survive only four or five days without it; and Gratitude because gratitude for everything in our lives keeps us dynamically alive, appreciating every breath of life. After these three essential components, there are twelve more fundamental practices that can be addressed in various orders, including sleep, play, rest, nutrition, elimination, intimacy, forgiveness, wealth, self-massage, service, movement and celebration. How you arrange these elements is entirely up to you. Your personal practice is your responsibility on the path to self-mastery. Every action, every feeling, thought and communion with spirit emits a resonance and an attraction.

So this, in a general way, has been the foundation for the curriculum I developed, and it continued to get better every day. Even as it got better, my school never got bigger. As I look back, I realize my natural, albeit unconscious, plan was show up to "work" each day and have fun. Now I realize I had created a work space where I had to do everything myself, and so the school couldn't grow.

Not long ago, my friend — JP, who'd been very involved with Wealth Dynamics — encouraged me to take the Wealth Dynamics profile test. I did, and discovered I was a Creator and Mechanic. I didn't know how to make more sense of it, or maybe I just wasn't ready to hear it, so I didn't follow through. Then, when a Japanese medical school asked if I wanted to sell my massage school, I knew instantly it was the right move, and in April, 2008, I did. To aid the transition, I still came to school every day, and during this time I had an epiphany: I was closing a chapter and ready to reinvent myself. I had focused on the school one hundred percent for twenty years and was really good at it, but it was no longer my passion and not the best use of my time and energy. I immediately phoned JP about my epiphany. We talked about my profile, and that's when I started to delve more deeply into Wealth Dynamics. It has changed my life. Before this understanding, I did everything at my school. I loved being in control of things, and I just assumed I had to do everything myself.

Wealth Dynamics set me free, showing me that I don't have to do everything; in fact, it's not wise for me to do everything, because it stalls expansion. My job, as Creator/Mechanic, is to generate ideas and facilitate structure, so other people will be inspired to come in and co-create a more magnificent expression. This epiphany is amazingly freeing. It allows me to move forward with my mission to spread Radical Self Care in so many ways. Wealth Dynamics reminds me that I am committed to attracting people who will shine their mastery on the aspects of a business that I'm best not doing. This understanding gives me the emotional freedom for self-mastery, the mastery of Radical Self Care.

When you are strong, healthy and grounded, you are of the greatest service.

I marvel at how perfectly Radical Self Care dovetails with Wealth Dynamics. Radical Self Care requires responsibility to oneself, first, and my Wealth Dynamics profile allowed me to move into a more focused, dynamic version of myself. Radical Self Care asks me to nurture what makes me happy and healthy and to let go of old attachments and distractions. The Wealth Dynamics profile shows clearly where our natural strengths shine. Not until I delved into Wealth Dynamics did I fully see how my life could flow when I just do what's natural, which means following my passions, and doing what gives me the most pleasure, the most charge. "Me first!" is my new mantra for self-care. We are always choosing, and when we are in flow, we can make the choice to focus on self. Saying, "Me first!" is not selfish; it is a declaration of love.

There are many ways that Radical Self Care and Wealth Dynamics are in perfect alignment, but there's one way that may be the most important: I believe deeply in service and paying it forward in our world as perpetual philanthropy.

Perpetual philanthropy means keeping our resources in flow. Resources are our wealth: our wealth of ideas, love, vegetables, smiles — everything that makes us healthy and happy.

We are designed to be stewards of our planet. The Hawaiians believe that we don't own anything, but are simply entrusted to care for things. Everything that is given to us is a gift entrusted to us. Our job (J.O.B. = Joy of Being) is to use it wisely, then pass the essence of that gift along.

The more fun you're having, the more inclined you are to give freely; and the more you give, the more fun you have. A core belief of Wealth Dynamics is in the links between contribution, contentment and fun. My personal program of Radical Self Care is a dynamic mix of self-care, which invariably leads to more connection, more contribution, more contentment. When you are strong, healthy and grounded, you are of the greatest service.

Wealth Dynamics helped elevate a unique awareness of myself and reveal a deeper understanding of Radical Self Care as a conscious path to health and happiness. Wealth Dynamics also guides me with innovative ways to collaborate. Radical Self Care delves into the mysteries of who you are and explores what it takes on a daily basis to design and maintain a healthy, happy, productive lifestyle on a daily basis. Start now! What could you possibly be waiting for?

Elizabeth Reveley is an international trainer, coach and expert in the sacred healing arts. Since 1984, when she opened The American Institute of Massage Therapy in Kailua, Hawaii, she has devoted her career and personal evolution to simplifying, synthesizing and sharing the sacred laws of the universe in the most practical possible way: self healing. She is the co-founder and director of Creative Life Resources, Inc., a not-for-profit educational and research foundation committed to promoting "self-care health-care" and the designer and developer of www.MyRadicalSelfCare.com. You can join her blog at www.ElizabethReveley.wordpress.com.

Warriors with a Noble Purpose

SANDRA EPSTEIN

Whether you are aware of it or not, all elements in nature are connected. Both modern science and ancient mysticism confirm our interdependent reality. We are all active parts of the whole universe; there is no separation between you and me, between the ocean and the sky, or between the man-made world and the natural world. This means that, even though you may be thousands of miles away from the Atlantic rainforest — my home — and never visit Brazil or set foot on the rainforest's floor, you are nevertheless an essential part of it. Indeed, in a connected world all the different elements add potency and beauty to the whole. In the living domain, richness of species and biodiversity enable a completely new set of possibilities. Moreover, each individual element is unique and multidimensional. A tree is not just a tree. It is an intricate living organism. A person is not just a person, but an elegant living being operating on many levels and connected to all there is and ever was. Every one of your emotions, actions and thoughts form a unique inner ecology, one that can be as complex as the biodiversity of the rainforest.

The biodiversity principle also applies to our society. It provides us with a tremendous opportunity to initiate transformation through building a society with less separation and judgment and more appreciation, collaboration and synergy.

Some of you may even say this transformation is happening now, and that entrepreneurs are at the forefront of the movement. They have a set of attributes — adventurous spirit, innovative vision, the courage to challenge the status quo and the ability to impact the economy — that makes them uniquely qualified to impart new possibilities, introduce new solutions and bring forth new dimensions to the planet. Entrepreneurs, who serve our society and help it reach its potential, are warriors with a noble purpose.

You are also such a warrior, as your vision is a necessary part of the whole. At first glance, your dream may seem small and insignificant; but it might change the world if it remains connected to the dreams of others and the collective dream of our society. To realize this dream, however, you will have to embrace the idea of the interdependence of all things, including the interconnectedness within yourself. Our education and conditioning systematically lead us toward fragmentation, in direct opposition to the natural world. We are compelled to see the separation of things around us and to hide behind multiple personas to protect us from the world "out there." This fragmented view distorts our perceptions of the world and obstructs our possibility for self-development, thus seriously inhibiting our potential for health, wealth and success on all levels. My life's work consists of gently challenging this fragmented worldview, and helping people establish a profound connection between who they are and what they do. Ever since my adolescence, I have seen the importance of education and the use of creativity in learning. I studied art and education at University, and later, with great curiosity, explored neuroscience.

Entrepreneurs, who serve our society and help it reach its potential, are warriors with a noble purpose.

My purpose, though, became clear in my thirties, when my dear friend John visited me in Ubatuba (my hometown on the Atlantic coast, just south of São Paulo). He arrived to die. Afflicted by a terrible cancer, he'd been given just three months to live. I felt committed to helping him overcome his pain and the shocking prospect of death. Every day, John and I strolled into the Atlantic rainforest. After a few days of enjoying nature, we took a new path that brought us to a hidden natural temple formed by majestic trees and a river flowing a long way from the mountains. The whole richness of the Atlantic rainforest was suddenly reflected in the atmosphere of this magical place. Admiring the trees, and the richness of life interconnected through this ecosystem, I had a profound insight. I clearly experienced that there was no separation between us and the flowers, the trees or the birds singing in the background. Not only did this magical environment awaken me to my calling; it also turned out to provide deep healing for John, who is, twenty years later, still alive and well.

We can easily understand that if we don't exercise, our muscles atrophy and our bodies deteriorate and get stuck while accommodating habitual postures and movements. The same is true for our emotions.

Over the years, in my devotion to helping people grow and experience their power to fulfill their dreams and contribute to society, I integrated my knowledge of and experience in art, education and neuroscience with field research and immersion in the rainforest. The resulting system of flower essences and practices I created — Ararêtama — taps directly into the world's greatest biodiversity, the Atlantic rainforest, to support deep human transformation and emotional liberation. The Ararêtama system helps balance out our inner biodiversity — emotional, mental and physical — by enhancing our brain plasticity (the brain's natural ability to learn and adapt).

We can easily understand that if we don't exercise, our muscles atrophy and our bodies deteriorate and get stuck while accommodating habitual postures and movements. The same is true for our emotions. If we spend years habitually reacting to events in the same way, we become stuck in experience and inflexible in behavior. Emotional fitness is thus critical for entrepreneurs to open up and expand flow.

When I discovered Wealth Dynamics while travelling in Europe a few years ago, the way I operated and experienced my work changed dramatically. I realized that, over many years as an entrepreneur, I had done everything myself — covering all the bases of my business and greatly compromising my Creator profile energy. So I stopped, and invested in building partnerships and an international team instead. For the first time in fifteen years, I was free to focus on design, research and innovation at home in Brazil. I knew I had found a powerful approach and tool-set for entrepreneurs to combine with Ararêtama, and put my creative energy into looking for practical ways to allow other entrepreneurs to be in flow too. I quickly understood that knowing the Wealth Dynamics profile is a revealing map for people who want to discover their best path toward wealth and self-expression — but it is often only the beginning. In my work, I have been engaged with entrepreneurs operating at different levels of wealth and stages of business who require both stepping into their profiles and being able to access the other energies.

Regardless of your profile, creating and contributing true wealth is neither an isolated game nor an individual sport. It requires accessing, understanding and integrating all five energies. This way, one can better understand and collaborate with others, grow while experiencing and expanding one's flow, and achieve better performance.

Like the flow in nature, there is a flow that runs through all eight Wealth Dynamics profiles. If you open up, you will be able to feel this flow within yourself and with others.

To support entrepreneurs, I partnered with Bea Benkova, Wealth Dynamics Master Practitioner in the UK, to practically connect Wealth Dynamics with Ararêtama. I developed specific programs and flower essences for each of the five energies and eight profiles, and created a special line of essences for empowering the extraordinary women Bea works with on their journeys of purpose.

Like the flow in nature, there is a flow that runs through all eight Wealth Dynamics profiles. If you open up, you will be able to feel this flow within yourself and with others. This approach enables people to expand their comfort zones and increase their emotional flexibility, thus opening up the gates for increased flow. It allows Stars, for example, to find grounding for their ambitions and deal with mechanical systems by accessing Trader and Mechanic energies. Lords, who need to improve their communication, are aided in a very simple way by exploring Supporter energy.

One of my clients, a Mechanic profile, naturally loves improving things and tinkering with systems — alone. That is her flow. But it is also part of her purpose to collaborate with people and develop teams to share her work. Using Ararêtama essences for Supporter and Deal Maker profiles, she began to open up, formed working groups and even began teaching in her area of expertise. Embracing and developing these aspects of herself, she tapped into increased flow as a Mechanic.

Similar principles apply for all profiles in each of the various stages of a business or a project. The Wealth Mandala program allows you to see the whole picture from the perspective of all profiles, and to begin accessing the frequencies you don't normally access, all without abandoning your profile. From this different point of view, you can see your natural role and course of action at each stage. Moreover, when you are in flow, your vibration creates resonance that attracts the right people to your project or business — those that will really help it succeed.

One thing I have noticed about the entrepreneurs and extraordinary women I encounter is that they become the lights, the shining stars in their communities. They have the courage to brighten themselves up and give at their full potential. And, equally important, they have the generosity to brighten others so that they can shine together. They don't build networks; they build glowing constellations that energize communities and brighten society for everyone's benefit. Ararêtama is an indigenous name meaning "the place from where the light comes." It is my legacy and my contribution to a shining world in which everyone plays an important part.

There is more to you than you realize, and there is space for everyone. You add something unique to the biodiversity of life that opens up a whole new world of possibilities for all of us. The world needs you to shine. Be the warrior with a noble purpose.

A native of Brazil, Sandra Epstein is an educator, entrepreneur, researcher and artist with a profound connection to the natural world. She has spent the last twenty years developing the Ararêtama Emotional Fitness system, a revolutionary personal evolution program integrating the principles of neuroscience and holistic education with the unique vibrational essences extracted from the rich flora of the Brazilian Atlantic rainforest. Through her innovative personal coaching, self-development workshops and choreographed group dancing, Sandra empowers business leaders and entrepreneurs all over the world to transform old limited patterns of thinking and behavior and build new lives of vibrant health and abundant wealth. She also works with specialized therapists who are helping children and their families overcome traumatic events. To learn more about Sandra, visit www.Araretama.com.br.

Finding Your True Purpose

ALISTAIR LOBO

The Oxford English Dictionary states that purpose is "The reason something exists." So — what is the reason you exist? Is there a more profound question you could possibly ask yourself? Is there anything more important to understand than your purpose?

I had a client, Eddie, whose dream was to walk into a Ferrari showroom, plunk down a suitcase full of cash, point to a yellow Ferrari and say, "I'm having that one," before he got the keys and drove away. He focused much of his life on that dream, and it came true before he was thirty (he actually paid with a banker's draft). Eddie got his yellow Ferrari and had a lot of fun driving around in it. For a few hours. But when he finished driving, Eddie returned home to an empty flat. His first wife had left him five years before, taking along his two children whom he hadn't seen in three years, and his second wife had recently left him. He felt completely empty inside, so he picked up his mobile phone and scrolled through his contacts in search of a true friend. Out of two hundred names, he found one friend, a guy named George.

He phoned George and told him about his purchase and how he now felt empty inside. "I've always wanted to ask," George said. "Why did you want the Ferrari?" Eddie recalled when he was fifteen years old, a time when he felt like a ship without a rudder. He was in the waiting area of a hair salon and a guy nearby was reading a magazine. On the back of that magazine was a picture of yellow Ferrari. "And that did it for me," Eddie said. George responded, "You actually made that yellow Ferrari your life's purpose." Eddie did something that we all do, on certain levels: we put something in a box that isn't really our spiritual purpose, and then we pursue that thing, thinking it will bring us happiness and fulfillment.

Our true spiritual purpose lies within, waiting for us to connect with it.

As a consultant and coach, I have worked with so many clients who have suffered all kinds of stress — some who have even attempted suicide — simply because there was something in their box that didn't belong there. That thing might have been a material object, or maybe someone else's dream, but whatever it was, it didn't relate to that person's spiritual purpose, their true purpose. You cannot begin to identify what should be in your box until you understand what your true purpose is. There is no bigger question you can answer in your life than what your true purpose is, because your true purpose is the reason you exist.

Your true purpose is also unique to you. The quantum physicist Wolfgang Pauli won a Nobel Prize for his theory, which concluded that no two atoms in the entire universe are exactly the same. So how could two people have exactly the same personality, values or purpose? My own ultimate purpose is the journey of growing my love for everyone, including myself. Pursuing that purpose is both my life's mission and the mission of my business: to empower organizations and people to get clarity on their own true purpose by connecting to the deepest part of who they are — and thus to lead inspiring and fulfilling lives. Your true purpose is your pathway to fulfillment. Success is a label that people put on other people. You only feel successful if you are fulfilled, and the only true path to fulfillment is through your purpose.

There is no bigger question you can answer in your life than what your true purpose is, because your true purpose is the reason you exist.

I use Wealth Dynamics to help people discover their spiritual purpose. My fulfillment-based approach to helping others is a pyramid. Wealth Dynamics is the square base of that pyramid. Each side forms the what, who, when and how, and the top of the pyramid is the WHY — the purpose. Wealth Dynamics, which is based on the I Ching, the ancient Chinese book of spiritual wisdom, helps me identify for others how they really are. Once they have a better sense of that, they can get a clearer picture of where they should go next.

One client, Jon Robson, came to me three years ago saying he had a lack of clarity about his life and was looking for a higher purpose. We clarified his inspiring purpose. Around this time he took up Kung Fu, and I also coached him on having an "effective mindset." Now he is the current Kung Fu British Champion, and I am presently working with him on his mindset training in readiness for the world championships in Montreal.

Your true purpose is inspiring. And when you have an inspiring purpose, you don't need any motivation. The word "inspiration" comes from roots that translate to "in spirit;" being inspired means being in spirit. Jon was inspired every day to work on his Kung Fu, because that's where his spirit wanted him to be. Inspiration takes you beyond motivation. Motivation is an external force, one that makes you feel obliged to do something; when you are inspired you jump out of bed, excited to do what you get to do that day.

Your true purpose is your pathway to fulfillment. Success is a label that people put on other people. You only feel successful if you are fulfilled, and the only true path to fulfillment is through your purpose.

Your true purpose increases flow and energy and reduces stress and effort, reaping greater results whether you are an individual or organization. In my own business, I have Deal Makers who act as my agents, getting me to my audiences and clients, and Supporters, Traders and Lords who conduct the marketing, handle customer service and manage my finances. This leverage through my team frees me to focus on shining on and magnifying my real value and passion, which is to guide others to their true purpose.

One result of those measures is that my Deal Makers have increased my earnings by several times in the last year alone. That success wasn't about me, per se. It was about me realizing I am a Star with a Creator wing and that, as far as possible, it's best to delegate those tasks that take me out of my flow.

Your true purpose is also always evolving. As you grow and develop, your purpose grows and develops. Your purpose is ever-increasing, and gives you a pathway of continuous upward movement and transformation. You may fall off or get lost, but if you are following your true purpose you will be growing and transforming. And, your true purpose exists beyond you or any part of your life. Most people have a purpose defined by environment and circumstances, but your purpose must be so overarching that it would be your purpose whether you were living in Auschwitz or in Beverly Hills with fifty million dollars in your bank account! If your purpose is dependent on your environment, then it is a mission or a goal, not your purpose! It is in fact your purpose that will inspire you to achieve any mission or goal that is congruent with your purpose. This is the gateway to fulfillment. But the single, most important overriding principle of your true purpose is that it will always lead you to love.

So what happened to Eddie, the guy with the yellow Ferrari? After a few sessions with me, he uncovered an inner purpose that brought him to tears of inspiration. And he also learned that he was living the life of a Trader when in fact he was a Star. He learned that a strong part of his spiritual essence was that of a teacher! He now teaches companies how to sell more effectively by being authentic and ethical, and he works only with organizations that deal with products people truly believe in.

> *The single, most important overriding principle of your true purpose is that it will always lead you to love.*

And the yellow Ferrari? He traded it in after his third coaching session with me. He used the money to pay for a course to learn what exactly he wanted to teach. Because he loves what he does, Eddie is one of the best in his field, and he now earns more than he ever did in his previous life. More important to Eddie is the feeling of fulfillment he gets at work — and most of all when he drives his two children and his golden retriever to the park in his relatively modest BMW Estate.

Alistair Lobo is an inspired performance coach for business leaders, as well as a speaker, writer and trainer. During his twenty-five-year business career, Alistair managed several small businesses before becoming project manager for the BBC and Siemens, working at board level on the largest IT media projects in the history of both organizations. As project manager, he rescued several multi-million dollar projects, turning them from "critical failure" to "successful delivery." His proudest business achievement was also his smallest management project, in which he delivered a three-million-pound project with a budget of only sixteen-thousand pounds, with a clear vision and purpose.

Alistair's mission is to show business leaders how to increase their performance levels while also increasing their levels of personal fulfillment. During the course of this journey he dedicated himself to researching, learning and applying the most advanced and leading-edge mindset and communication technologies, and applying them in the workplace to get measurable results. Alistair is an active practitioner, trainer and facilitator in many fields, including spiral dynamics, EFT, neuro-linguistic programming (NLP), hypnotherapy and neuro-strategies, the Demartini method® and Wealth Dynamics. For more information about Alistair, visit www.AlistairLobo.com or www.CertainProgress.com.

Turn Your Passion into Cash Flow Today

FRANCES CHEUNG WITH ALLAN CHEUNG

I used to believe it was impossible to combine passion with cash inflow. However, after I discovered how easy it was to actually turn passion into cash flow, I threw that old belief out the window and discovered my purpose in business: to inspire and educate people to do only what they love and be extremely rich in doing so.

Today, I'm known as the "WISE Lady" (Wealth Insights Serving Entrepreneurs). When I first started out at university, becoming an entrepreneur was not part of the plan. Like most people, what I was after was a high-paying job. At the time, engineering graduates got paid the most; so even though I didn't love it one hundred percent, I studied for and graduated with a degree in electrical engineering. Six years later, getting an MBA was hot, so I got an MBA from Northwestern University's Kellogg Graduate School of Management. With two degrees and a burning desire to succeed, I was on the career fast track: I worked as an engineer, a consultant, and then as a senior executive for multi-national companies. What I got was a big house, fancy cars, a loving husband and two wonderful children. Yet, while my life seemed to be perfect, I struggled to get up in the morning.

Working overtime and unintentionally ignoring my health and my family had made me miserable. My husband Allan, who enjoyed a very successful career as an entrepreneur, also felt miserable. It became clear to us that, while we just had to stay on that path for a few more years to become CEOs or VPs of listed companies, neither of us was willing to sacrifice personal and family well-being in order to get there. So we both walked away from our jobs.

Fast-forward five years, to today. I absolutely love what I do. Allan and I have created five new businesses and achieved financial freedom. Through our Work*Play at Karisma Learning Institute, we teach clients exactly how to turn their passion into cash flow — whether they already have a business, are just starting out or never want to run one. We no longer work. We play. Our vocation has indeed become our vacation, and our mission is to simply share this newfound reality with a million entrepreneurs globally.

Here is a snapshot of our life now: we're growing a young family and multiple businesses; swimming and playing ping pong with our kids; going on diving holidays and retreats with clients who've become close personal friends; and learning, teaching and connecting with amazing people.

Five years ago, we could *never* have imagined how much joy we could feel doing our work, or how fast our business would take off. What we discovered and now teach to all our clients is so simple that you'll likely find it too obvious: when you choose work that is aligned with your Wealth Dynamics profile and with what you love to do, work feels easy, natural and very exciting — like play.

> *We no longer work. We play. Our vocation has indeed become our vacation, and our mission is to simply share this newfound reality with a million entrepreneurs globally.*

Wealth Dynamics is a core component of our Passion to Cash Flow process because it is an excellent tool for discovering who you are, and where you are. Too often people make education, career and business decisions based on trends or perceived economic viability, just as I did. Greg, one of our success stories, had a similar challenge. An employee of a large company, he was able to support his family and his lifestyle, but his job was just a way to make a living.

When Greg came to me, I could see that one of his biggest challenges was his BUSY-ness. His job took a big chunk of his time. In his free time, he was occupied with real estate investments, Internet marketing and options trading.

None of these pursuits actually produced income; worse still, he wasn't sure if any of them aligned with his true passion in life. Taking Greg through the Passion to Cash Flow process, I helped him get clear about his passion in two areas: clean water for everyone on the planet and empowering people to be their best. In working with me, he was able to see how he could leverage his natural Supporter abilities and Blaze energy to create more cash flow from his passions and to do it simply.

Within twelve months, Greg increased his net income by nearly three thousand percent. He finally connected the dotted line between his job and his passion, and while still employed with the same company, his workday now feels playful because he no longer sees his job as work.

Today, Greg only accepts invitations to opportunities that resonate with his passions, instead of being too busy accepting all good opportunities that come his way. He has gained so much free time that he now focuses on becoming an expert in his field, and regularly speaks and writes on the subjects of clean water and being your best. He attracts the right people and opportunities magically, at the right time. Within twelve months, Greg increased his net income by nearly three thousand percent. He finally connected the dotted line between his job and his passion, and while still employed with the same company, his workday now feels playful because he no longer sees his job as work.

I met Sam, another client, when he attended my courses in Hong Kong. He had just quit his job at a prestigious multinational company because he no longer felt happy in it. A few months later, I met up with Sam again. He had not generated much income in the past year and was considering going back to work. I told him not to give up, and invited him to play with the Passion to Cash Flow process. In just a few weeks, we defined Sam's Primary Income Game (PIG) based on his primary passion. With a repositioned personal branding message, Sam was able to take on a few projects as technical advisor to companies that found his expertise valuable, but could not afford to hire him full time. Sam earned enough from his PIG to meet his expenses, and now uses his extra time to turn all of his other passions into cash flow streams as well. Sam recently told me, "It feels like one big river of cash flow; I totally love 'working' through the Passion to Cash Flow process."

Greg's and Sam's stories are far too common. In 2005, Harris Interactive found that only twenty percent of working Americans were passionate about what they were doing. And guess what? Small business owners have an even tougher time. In our work, we've discovered that most start by doing what they love as a "solo-preneur" and end up feeling their business is just another job that owns them, sucks up all their time and energy and gives little money in return. What's causing this problem we all face? Five main obstacles prevent people from turning Passion into Cash Flow now:

1. Believing that it is impossible to do only what you love and be extremely rich doing so. As a result, people take on work that they are not suited to, and wait for evenings or weekends to have fun. Since belief determines actions and actions lead to outcomes, this belief will always be true for those who have it.

2. Lacking clarity in passion. Most people are aware that they are not happy at work, but few know exactly what they love to do. Clarity begets confidence, empowering you to take action; your confidence also inspires others to know exactly how to support you in living your passion.

3. Carrying the baggage of prior education and training. A lot of people choose an education path based on income potential. Then they build an attractive resumé, showing an accumulation of work experience in that area. People get stuck, torn between these prior investments in time and energy and new careers more in line with their passion.

4. Failing to commercialize their passion. Many entrepreneurs fail to run their passion-based projects as businesses. Sometimes this is because they don't have much business experience. Other times, they simply don't know how to charge properly for the services they provide. In either case, they do what they love and still lack the cash flow to let them do more of what they love on an ongoing basis.

5. Trying to do it on their own. Most who are courageous enough to pursue their passion as an income game fail to find a team to ensure its success. We tend to forget that "no one can do it alone." Think of professional athletes. They could not have turned their hobby or passion into highly profitable careers without their teams of agents and coaches (and in some cases, fellow team players), could they?

In our Work*Play, we work with people to take apart all of these obstacles. You can model our process by first thinking in terms of What is Possible (WIP) instead of thinking, "I cannot leave my job." Then, play with new WIPs, such as, "I can make millions doing what I love." Next, identify what you love to do, something you would be willing to devote your life to with or without pay. Using Wealth Dynamics, discover and get clarity about who you are and where you are.

A true master continues learning, improving and practicing, even after the money comes rolling in.

Now where does the cash flow come from? It comes from defining your income games. Before your Passion to Cash (P2C) game produces a cash flow, keep your PIG that brings in the bacon. Keep track of your personal monthly expenses so you put just enough time into your PIG to finance your current lifestyle, and invest the rest of your time, energy and focus in playing the P2C game.

Finally, find a mentor who does what you'd love to do and is already turning his passion into cash flow. Expand your support network by joining a team of players with a passion similar to yours, people who are already playing their P2C game. With this foundation, system and team in place, it's time to practice, practice, practice. A true master continues learning, improving and practicing, even after the money comes rolling in.

Why do we use sports as a metaphor? Because people understand sports. In sports, every type of game has its rules. Understanding the rules helps us to play the game and win. Once we know the rules, we start to play and to find our best, most natural position on the playing field. We practice, get better, keep practicing — and eventually, we get paid to play professionally. Just as with sports, this is how it works in business and in life. Are you ready to play?

Directors of the Hong Kong-based Karisma Learning Institute, avid investors and travelers Frances and Allan Cheung developed and teach the successful Passion Into Cash Flow (P2C) process.

Known as the #1 WISE lady (Wealth Insights Serving Entrepreneurs) in China, Frances is a Wealth Dynamics Master Practitioner and the Lead Trainer (2008) for the Wealth Dynamics Institute. Her traditional work experience includes six years in manufacturing at General Motors and Johnson & Johnson and six years in telecommunications marketing and business development at Motorola. To learn more about Frances and Allan, and to find more resources to support you on your journey to turn passion into cash flow, visit www.AskFrancesToday.com.

Alignment = Attraction

JO WARD

Everyone's talking about the Law of Attraction. We're right to be thrilled about the fact that the universe conspires with our deepest desires and beliefs to help us live our highest purpose. The strength that awareness of our own belief systems brings to our ability to manifest happiness, health and wealth is creating a sea change in the world of personal transformation and business success. The best way to honor this knowledge is to make sure we use the Law of Attraction to manifest the opportunities, objects and relationships that are in the closest alignment with our highest purpose.

In my work with clients in one-to-one coaching sessions and in my Star-appropriate role as a trainer and public speaker, the Law of Attraction is a phenomenon I *always* speak about. It's huge, and access to it is absolutely key to leading a fulfilling, joyful life. The Law of Attraction is based on the simple idea that we draw toward us that which we truly believe we deserve and desire. Great! Easy enough, right? All we have to do to live the life of our dreams, then, is to repeat a mantra to ourselves, a picture of our ideal, and it will magically materialize.

Well, there's a little more to it than that. The Law of Attraction doesn't just work through conscious thought processes. It also works via the unconscious mind, whose projections are just as powerful as those of the conscious mind. You may say to yourself, for instance, that you want to be successful in business, be your own boss and expand from a small operation to an international franchise in five years. But what if your unconscious mind, fettered by old patterns of feeling fearful and unworthy, has something else to say?

The first step to fully participating with the dynamism of the Law of Attraction is clearing your unconscious mind of self-limiting and negative thoughts. Then, and only then, can the ideals of the conscious mind come into full alignment with the power of unconscious messages. Put simply, one's conscious and unconscious minds need to be speaking the same language. If they're not, the universe hears static instead of a clear message stating what you want. It's like that experience we've all had of standing between two people at a party who are each speaking loudly, and at the same time. It's impossible to really comprehend what is being said — by either of them. On the other hand, when the conscious and unconscious are speaking the same message, in the same language, the universe registers the message without fail and goes to work immediately to deliver it — fast.

I've done a lot of work with my own unconscious belief systems to come to a point where I can really take advantage of the power of the Law of Attraction. Now it flows through my life in a way that consistently delights and surprises me. And as the seeming synchronicity continues to increase in frequency, my conscious and unconscious belief in its endless possibilities grows. Movement can occur when all parts of the self are in alignment with each other. Anything that can be imagined can be accomplished.

The first step to fully participating with the dynamism of the Law of Attraction is clearing your unconscious mind of self-limiting and negative thoughts.

Some time ago, I decided I wanted to learn to play the guitar. A particular, beautiful melody had caught my attention and I wanted to make the sound myself. So I asked a friend of mine, who worked in a charity-based thrift store, if she ever saw a guitar come in. "Oh, no," she said. "I've worked here for a year and a half, and I've never seen one." "Okay," I said. "When one comes in tomorrow, give me a ring." My friend called the next morning, laughing in disbelief. "Guess what just walked in here!" she cried. "Your guitar!" This was my "aha!" moment with the Law of Attraction. And my belief in it has grown ever since. It wasn't second nature at first, though. I had to rewire my unconscious thoughts.

The Law of Attraction always delivers, though not always in the form you expect! So be specific in your language — the more detail the better. Let your values work in line with your beliefs, toward what you want! Remove blocks, old beliefs and values and negative emotions that are no longer serving you. This will increase your vibration so you have a clearer, stronger connection to the universe. You now have a personal radio station that is fine-tuned to play the song you want to attract into your life. Choose wisely!

That's just the beginning of the story, however. The other key to unlocking the potential of the Law of Attraction is being in profile, in flow.

I've helped clients break through negative patterns for years. I first met one of my clients, an electrician, when he came to rewire my house. It struck me that we do similar work: he rewires buildings; I rewire minds. I spoke this observation aloud to him and he said, "Do you think you could help rewire me? I'm angry at my children, feel guilty for the death of my father, addicted to sugar, concerned with my health, and my business is a mess." I gladly agreed, and after fifteen minutes together, in our first session, we had cleared the dog phobia he'd had since age seven!

Next, we worked on clearing his deeply held negative thought patterns. In a very short time, he was able to drop his sugar habit, get healthier and find more space to enjoy life. His business is now thriving and attracting lots of clients, and his family has started enjoying each other again. Now he raves about having totally transformed his life, and he is even fencing the garden to have a dog for his kids!

That's just the beginning of the story, however. The other key to unlocking the potential of the Law of Attraction is being in profile, in flow. When I discovered Wealth Dynamics, I realized I'd been missing an essential piece of the Law of Attraction. How can we know what we really want and need if we don't understand ourselves first? Without a foundation for self-knowledge, we may end up attracting things, relationships and achievements that are not in alignment with our highest purpose on this planet, or our true natures. We may find ourselves playing a game or a role that doesn't suit who we are, and causing ourselves a lot of stress in the process.

The Wealth Dynamics profile is the perfect tool for clarifying our easiest routes to success. This tool enables us to open our flow to receive, via the Law of Attraction, what will truly serve the highest good. Knowing my Star profile, I'm acutely aware of my talents and needs. I need stage, interaction, sparkle and lots of people. Whatever I ask for from the Universe, now, is based in that irreplaceable knowledge of myself.

The Law of Attraction has to work with the big picture of who a person is — the profile — just as it has to come through the clear and complementary channels of the conscious and unconscious mind. The Law of Attraction and Wealth Dynamics go hand in hand. To find true alignment, communicate with your unconscious mind and look to your profile before you ask the Universe to deliver! And give thanks every day.

Jo Ward is a social entrepreneur, transformational speaker, trainer and life coach with certification as a trainer and Master Practitioner of NLP, Time Line Therapy®, Hypnosis and Wealth Dynamics. A Star who attracts other Stars as clients, she has become an expert on the dynamics of the Star profile. Before setting up her own business, Jo was highly successful in the fashion and retail sector as a global marketer and business development specialist. She brings this expertise to her transformational speaking and workshop sessions with corporations, organizations and individual clients. To learn more about Jo, visit www.Jo-Ward.com.

Top Performance
from Teams at the Top

RICHARD WINFIELD

Not so long ago the Operations Manager of a national standards organization was appointed to its Board of Directors. He was a caring man and had worked his way to the top. But when a new CEO was hired two years later, he pointed out that the former Operations Manager was not playing his role as a Director. I was called in to coach him in his new role. When directors are first appointed they often have difficulty adapting to their new role. They have problems dealing with their legacy relationships and can be tempted to waste a lot of time demanding too much information, or they can be shy of asking "naïve" questions. This is where an independent intermediary can save a lot of time at induction by helping a new director establish new rules and relationships.

My client had been an effective Operations Manager because he concentrated on his team, its well-being and how together they could meet the goals set for them. He was the "mother hen," making sure team members had the tools they needed to perform their tasks. As all good managers do, he focused downward within the firm. But the tasks of an effective Director are quite different; a Director must focus upward and outward, not downward and inward. The move from being a manager to holding a directorship is more than a change in responsibility; it is a change in behavior and identity.

In one of my coaching exercises, my client asked his former staff what they expected of him as a Director. They told him they did not need him as a "mother hen." Instead, they wanted him to manage upwards, representing their interests but always contributing to the best interests of the firm as a whole. This response came as a shock to him, but it helped him let go of the viewpoint that had served him well as he climbed the corporate ladder. Once he refocused on his responsibility to the organization as a whole, he became an effective member of its Board of Directors. It also lowered the stress in his life, since he was able to work with his own strengths.

The move from being a manager to holding a directorship is more than a change in responsibility; it is a change in behavior and identity.

Because Directors and Boards determine strategy and overall planning, helping them become more effective is one of the quickest, surest ways of transforming an organization. Effective Directors and Boards are key to the long-term success of an organization; they have the most advantageous position from which to effect ongoing change for the business; they are accountable for providing strategic leadership, establishing and maintaining the culture and acting as role models and ambassadors for the rest of the organization. Yet many Boards lack effective processes.

An independent, impartial evaluation of Board effectiveness can quickly highlight where the Board needs to focus in order to maximize strengths and tackle weaknesses, leading to an immediate improvement in performance throughout the organization.

The starting point, of course, is to have the right Directors on the Board, and there should be a formal, rigorous and transparent procedure for the appointment of new Directors to the Board.

Board effectiveness depends not just on the experience, skill and judgment of individual executive and non-executive Directors, but also the ways in which these are combined and managed to shape Board conduct and relationships. However, there is ample evidence to demonstrate that many Boards are still selected and managed based on criteria that do not consistently deliver the necessary balance needed for the good governance and sound decision making that lead to sustained success. This has been borne out in recent years in a number of high profile corporate failures. Global Crossing, Enron and WorldCom are well known examples of this.

It always grieves me when well-known personalities are involved in corporate scandals that they had been unaware of. It is their primary responsibility as non-executive Directors to constructively challenge strategy, scrutinize performance and monitor the reporting of information. Directors are legally responsible and all Directors must satisfy themselves that financial information is accurate and that financial controls and systems of risk management are robust and defensible.

My study of Wealth Dynamics has provided me with added insights into my work with Boards. It's clear to me that the fundamental traits embodied in the eight Wealth Dynamics profiles can be seen clearly at work in organizations and their Boards. I've come to see why Boards can benefit from achieving a stronger balance, and therefore improved sustainable performance, by including members that provide a distributed mix of the eight Wealth Dynamics P profiles — as well as the relevant skills and experience. One of the key topical benefits of this type of composition is the ability of Boards to react more readily — and appropriately — to prevailing market conditions, at each stage of the company's growth.

Because Directors and Boards determine strategy and overall planning, helping them become more effective is one of the quickest, surest ways of transforming an organization.

One year, by coincidence, I was coaching the partners of two surveying companies. A land survey company had been started by three surveyors. They were all typical technical types and so were most of their staff. They were primarily from the "Steel" side of Wealth Dynamics and lacked the more extroverted and people-focused aspects of the "Blaze" side. To an outsider, the company was "worthy but boring." The other company was a quantity surveying firm; it had been founded by an ambitious entrepreneur who had recruited strongly in his own image. Here the culture was quite different. There was a lot of energy but projects and reports were completed at the very last minute with plenty of adrenalin and late hours. To an outsider, this company was "exciting but stressful." If these two companies had been able to interchange some of their Board members they might each have been much more successful — however, a merger between the two cultures would have been too big a step.

The good news is that adoption of best practice will enable Directors and Boards to significantly raise their game, improving both corporate governance and financial performance.

Too often in my experience, I find that Boards lack basic processes and controls to enable effective governance and strategic leadership. Unless they review at least annually how their strategy, culture and behavior align with their vision, mission and values, they can easily drift off course — and in this fast changing world, the course itself should be reviewed regularly. Exercises like this, as well as strategy planning, budgeting and scenario planning, require uninterrupted time away from the workplace in order to stimulate creativity. In the past, I have facilitated corporate retreats in the Rocky Mountains, a Texas ranch, an African game resort and many country hotels. The whole team is involved in analysis, creativity and action planning. By the end of the event, Directors have clarified and focused their thinking as well as strengthened their relationships, and they leave energized and motivated.

Board meetings are another focus of my work. For many companies, these meetings consume far too much time, are often badly managed and concentrate on the wrong matters. Too often, they are dedicated solely to an appraisal of recent performance of the organization, analyzing reports and dealing with problems.

A framework of clearly established standards of good practice enables all Directors, including non-executive Directors, to be appraised and supported with the professional development necessary to ensure optimum performance. The good news is that adoption of best practice will enable Directors and

Boards to significantly raise their game, improving both corporate governance and financial performance. I have seen time and again how "raising the bar" in this manner can make a decisive contribution to long-term business success.

And finally, it's worth noting that one of the thorniest topics over the past several years has been corporate accountability. This comes in various guises, ranging from accountability for strategy and financial performance to corporate social responsibility. However, when you strip back the theory and rhetoric, accountability is virtually always the real issue. Many Boards appear to be functioning in a very corporate, responsible way until put under the intense pressure of changing market conditions or revelations of significant financial difficulties that were previously unreported. This can often be traced back to an imbalance between Board members and, in a number of cases, an imbalance between a dominant CEO and the Board.

Once again, this is where Wealth Dynamics profiling can serve as a powerful tool for discovering individual Director's natural talent and ensuring that it is applied most appropriately within the team. This can lead to some change of roles or recruitment of additional directors. When the composition of the Board is right, implementing or strengthening appropriate processes can have a dramatic impact on effectiveness, not just at Board level, but also across the business.

The businesses that survive today's challenging environment are likely to be those that focus on tuning up their performance — at all levels. And since "everything rolls downhill," the Board is a great place to start!

Action Questions
- How effective is your Board?
- Are all your Board meetings efficient, effective and strategic?
- Do all your directors fully understand their role — and match up to best practice?
- When did you last review the processes, behaviors and skill sets of your Board directors against international standards?

Richard Winfield is a Wealth Dynamics Master Practitioner with a Mechanic profile. He is the founder of The Brefi Group (www.brefigroup.com), an international organization development consultancy based in Birmingham, UK. The Brefi Group helps individuals and teams in organizations discover and achieve their potential so that they become more effective with less stress. Richard consults, coaches and facilitates internationally, specializing in Directors and Boards in transition: helping them to make progress by bringing structure and clarity to their thinking. He also trains coaches to be able to work at the senior executive level and is co-founder of the Indian School of Executive Coaching.

Beyond Excuses
to Purposeful Flow

DAVE ROGERS

The discovery of Wealth Dynamics has led to great evolution in my life. Before I became aware that I was a Deal Maker, I acted as a Supporter, working as a corporate banker, a credit risk officer and a deputy general manager in Japan. Later, leaning into my Trader side, I traded Asian bonds and managed a billion-dollar US portfolio out of Hong Kong. Though I was not technically in flow, I did enjoy great success in those other roles. Part of the satisfaction I felt came from the feeling of stretching my own limits.

I found my true path when, after unintentionally orchestrating many happy marriages and other fruitful partnerships, I discovered I was a Deal Maker! It has been so rewarding to step into flow and enjoy my natural ability to help people connect at the right time and in the right place. But that doesn't mean that I've eliminated the traits and instincts that allowed me to achieve as a Supporter and a Trader; in fact, my early experiences playing my adjoining profile games have helped me support and connect with all profiles.

Wealth Dynamics gives us insights that allow us to appreciate and respect ourselves, and others, more deeply. When we are in flow, and witness others in flow, we can see individual attributes as strengths rather than frailties. Then we can surround ourselves with complementary profiles, people who are naturally good at what we struggle with. Awareness of our own dynamic allows a clear operating paradigm. The profile, however, is not to be used as an excuse mechanism. Far too often, I find that people use their Wealth Dynamics profile as an excuse not to grow, not to stretch or challenge themselves. For instance, a Creator with a strong Mechanic side may be more about finishing projects and having a system, as opposed to a Creator with a strong Star side, who will be out on stage at the drop of a hat. But that doesn't mean that either Creator should avoid developing new strengths in order to play at the top of his game. Our success has everything to do with the level at which we decide to take responsibility, exercise discipline and avoid the scourge of what I call "excusitis."

Observing yourself in a new element can allow you to stretch yourself.

Each of us loves our comfort zone; but the purpose of Wealth Dynamics is not to coddle us, it's to help us grow and contribute. The Creator-Mechanic, for example, can really stretch herself by consciously building her network to access support from different profiles, such as Deal Makers and Stars. In order to build a great team, she must emerge from her protective shell, rather than saying to herself, "I'm an introverted Creator-Mechanic; I don't leave the house."

You are suffering from excusitis if you're telling yourself something like, "I'm an Accumulator. I don't speak in front of people." What rubbish! You're cutting yourself off. Being able to share your message with confidence and certainty is of paramount importance. It adds value to you, your profile and whatever game you're playing. Look at Warren Buffet, a master Accumulator. He's an extremely articulate person who has invested time in learning to present publicly. And while it was a stretch, he knows it contributes to his growth as an individual.

One of the women I work with, Joy, is a great example of this. She's also an Accumulator and was a banker who really enjoyed her work. Her first read of the Accumulator profile was typical: an Accumulator doesn't go out much, doesn't talk much. But she didn't stop with that first look; she had a desire for growth so challenged herself instead.

Joy joined Toastmasters — clearly not a natural choice for an Accumulator! — and eventually became a leader of Toastmasters. (All profiles can learn to be compelling public speakers — as long as they do so in their own authentic style.) Soon after, she started her own event management company. Employing more extroverted people, particularly Supporter and Star profiles, allowed

Joy to complement her natural tendencies — like focusing on crunching numbers — with promoting the business and connecting with potential partners. She could have made excuses and become a hermit, hiding herself in her room, but instead she continued to work on herself. In fact, Joy became the events coordinator for the Global Speakers Summit in Singapore, where she was able to meet and form great relationships with many fantastic speakers, all of whom wanted her to promote them.

Observing yourself in a new element can allow you to stretch yourself. Wealth Dynamics is a wonderful, powerful tool. It does release us from ideas we may have held about what we "should" and "shouldn't" know, do or be. But that doesn't mean we should allow our profile to be an excuse. In Wealth Dynamics, as with everything that exists, there's a flip side, a yin and yang, a light and a dark side. If someone stays in the light, he can act as a messenger of the light; but if he's operating out of flow, he can actually go to the dark side of his Wealth Dynamics profile.

Making excuses and limiting ourselves because we imagine our profiles give us permission to do so is most definitely NOT being in flow.

Each profile has its dark side: for example, a Creator can create a magnificent, expansive vision when he's working in flow, or become an intense "control freak" who over-promises when he moves into stress, into the dark side of his profile.

Making excuses and limiting ourselves because we imagine our profiles give us permission to do so is most definitely NOT being in flow. All too often I've seen people use their profiles as a justification to ignore areas of their development that hold them back from playing their complete game and that keep them from recognizing how to fully leverage their profile. It's like Tiger Woods saying, "I don't need to practice," or Michael Jordan insisting, "I don't want to shoot free throws." Well, guess what? These guys practice whether they "feel like it" or not, knowing that these are essential components to their games. That's why they are great athletes. To be truly liberated by Wealth Dynamics, we need to do what challenges us to grow our ability to add value and contribute at the highest level. Each profile has a game to play, and it's part of an entrepreneur's toolkit to understand every aspect of how to play that game.

You don't have to do it all, but if you don't have accountability, you'll set yourself up for trouble. As entrepreneurs, we must understand and take responsibility for every role. This is an essential piece of being in flow and playing your best game. When that's what you're up to, you'll attract others who are playing their best games, too. Then, when you find someone who loves what they do, and their role isn't necessarily your strength, that's when the synergy really begins to come into play.

Most of us are aware of when we're not in flow, but what can we do to get there?

Accepting responsibility also means investing time and effort in understanding your keys to wealth creation. Read about successful wealth creators and how they've played their game. Talk to people you admire about their habits of thinking and learning. Check out books like *Your Life, Your Legacy*, which gives many examples of leaders who are successfully playing the games most appropriate to their Wealth Dynamics profiles. Then see where you can challenge yourself.

When I encountered my own dark side in the past, it most often showed itself as impatience with people who didn't think the way I did. Being in flow and acknowledging my own complex path has given me greater compassion, respect and love for everyone I encounter, regardless of profile.

Part of transcending excusitis is being aware that everyone we meet is a reflection of our own being. I know that if someone gets under my skin, he is likely a trigger for something in me that wants to come out of the darkness and move into the light. So if I choose to focus on blaming someone else for my frustration, I've allowed excusitis to usurp some important and potentially very illuminating territory.

Most of us are aware of when we're not in flow, but what can we do to get there? Living a life of curiosity is the opposite of wimping out by making excuses. Given all the elements of change whirling through our planet right now, it's no longer about just going out there and learning; we have entered an age of applied learning, applied wisdom. We must keep evolving, asking better questions, taking on new roles and re-engineering ourselves so that our relevance continues.

To do that, we need to let go of old constructs, ideas of who we are that limit us and that particular part of our past that holds us back, stays stuck and refuses to grow or apply new knowledge. Curiosity goes hand in hand with this process of letting go. Wealth Dynamics offers us a challenge, not a reason to lie down. Wealth Dynamics is about evolution.

Each profile has value. And each has a question it identifies with most — what, who, when, where and how — but the essential question for all profiles is, "Why?" Our "Why?" is our enterprise and/or life purpose. And if our "Why?" is big enough, excusitis simply cannot triumph over us. My biggest "Why?" is eradicating extreme poverty on this planet. That's a Why that really keeps me going. How about you? What's your Why? Find out — and then go for it. No excuses!

Dave Rogers is a keynote speaker, author and executive coach whose awards include "The Spirit of Enterprise," a prestigious honor in Singapore. A Deal Maker profile, Dave focuses on early-round fundraising and real estate investing primarily in developing markets. He has appeared on radio, television and stage in more than eighteen countries. A published writer, Dave is the author of two books including Awesome Coaching and several audio home study guides, including The Dealmaker's Guidebook, an indispensable resource for learning to work in harmony with every Wealth Dynamics profile. Learn more at www.DaveRogers.net, www.ContinualShift.com, and www.CoachDaveRogers.blogspot.com.

How Does
Your Garden Grow?

Success comes from knowing which game to play, and then playing that game
— and only that game.
                              — from Your Life, Your Legacy by Roger Hamilton

You now know that it's possible to create real, lasting wealth when you live and work in flow. You know too that to get into flow, you must first determine which game to play, the game that best suits your natural talents, interests and abilities. As exemplified by the remarkable co-authors of this book, a tremendous sense of freedom comes with discovering, claiming and honoring your natural gifts. When you walk your unique path to wealth creation, you will no longer seek success — success will find you.

As you read this book, perhaps you thought about how your team, your business, your life could flourish if you tapped into flow. Maybe, with every new chapter, you refined, clarified and expanded your entrepreneurial vision — a vision in closer alignment with your purpose. And we hope that now, as you read this last page, you feel ready to harness the transformative power of Wealth Dynamics.

So, how do you begin? How do you step into flow? How does your garden grow?

It begins with a profile. If you haven't done so already, visit The Wealth Garden website at www.TheWealthGarden.com to take the Wealth Dynamics profile assessment.

If you have taken the assessment and know your profile, visit *The Wealth Garden* website, and the websites found in our co-authors' bios. Reach out to the coaches, mentors, speakers, trainers, healers and consultants who contributed their stories, insight and wisdom to this book. They are all part of a thriving community of global gardeners, social entrepreneurs who welcome the opportunity to help you gain a deeper understanding of your own profile, build dynamic teams and realize your highest potential.

When you walk your unique path to wealth creation, you will no longer seek success — success will find you.

May you grow a garden that brings you joy, serves the greater good and attracts wealth and opportunities beyond your imagination.